MURDER&
MADNESS

MURDER&
MADNESS

THE SECRET LIFE OF
JACK THE RIPPER
by
David Abrahamsen, M.D.,
Fellow of the American College
of Psychoanalysts

DONALD I. FINE, INC.
New York

455427

Copyright © 1992 by David Abrahamsen

All rights reserved, including the right of reproduction in whole or in part
in any form. Published in the United States of America by Donald I. Fine,
Inc. and in Canada by General Publishing Company Limited.

Library of Congress Cataloging-in-Publication Data

Abrahamsen, David, 1903—
Murder & madness : the secret life of Jack the Ripper / David
Abrahamsen.
p.   cm.
Includes bibliographical references and index.
ISBN 1-55611-279-3
1. Jack the Ripper Murders, London (England) 1888.   I. Title.
II. Title: Murder and madness.
HV6535.G6L613   1992
364.1'523'092—dc20   91-58655
CIP

2. Homicide - London (England), 1888.

Manufactured in the United States of America

10 9 8 7 6 5 4 3 2 1

Designed by Irving Perkins Associates

Excerpts from *Virginia Woolf: A Biography,* copyright © 1972 by Quentin Bell,
and *Moments of Being* by Virginia Woolf, copyright © 1976
by Quentin Bell and Angelica Garnett, reprinted by permission of
Harcourt Brace Jovanovich, Inc.

Excerpts from *Jack the Ripper,* copyright © 1980 by Richard Gordon, reprinted
by permission of Curtis Brown, London, Ltd. on behalf of Richard Gordon.

For Lova—
the only one

Contents

Acknowledgments

DESPITE DAUNTING FRUSTRATIONS throughout the decade of my studies into the case of Jack the Ripper, I was finally able to uncover the historical, literary, psychiatric-psychocriminal and pathological material relating to the five Whitechapel murders in the autumn of 1888.

I am deeply grateful for the guidance I received from such august institutions as the Wellcome Institute for the History of Medicine in London, the British Library and the British Museum, both also in London, the Library of the New York Academy of Medicine, the New York Public Library and the Annex Library of New York. The assistance of their respective officers was invaluable in securing the information I needed for the exploration of the Ripper case.

Special thanks go to J. M. Cameron, M.D., Professor of Pathology, and to Bernard Simms, M.D., both of London Hospital Medical College. They provided me with valuable background material and information about the murderous events and opened the way for further exploration of the personal characteristics of the suspects. Further assistance came from William Eckert, M.D., of Wichita, Kansas.

Documents of the murders of 1888 abounded in the annals of Scotland Yard, later known as New Scotland Yard. I am grateful to London's investigative units for granting me access to the Public Record Offices and permitting me to review the police investigations and records of the inquests of the Whitechapel murders. Particular mention is deserved by A. V. Comben, Chief Superintendent Staff Officer to the Deputy Commissioner, who directed me to the Public Record Office, and to Miss A. Crawford of the Search Department, who diligently searched and eventually located the relevant documents in the Public Record Office in the Coroner's Court, as well as the local record office.

Two parcels were sent to me from the Public Record Office in London. Inside were 1,643 prints of the Complete Files of Jack the Ripper. Documents concerning inquests of two of the murdered women were missing, but were promptly forwarded following a simple request. I acknowledge James R. Sewell, M.A., F.S.A., the City Archivist at Guild Hall in London, for his prompt attention and subsequent permission to publish the pertinent material.

I am also grateful to John H. Henderson, M.D., Medical Director of St. Andrew's Hospital, Northampton, England, for his kindness in permitting me to review and publish information from the hospital records regarding one of the suspects in this book. The psychiatric record of this protagonist, written one hundred years ago, offers new insight into the extent of the illness underlying such fiendish murders.

I am thankful for the Monroe County Library in Key West, Florida, which facilitated the tracing of material in my research. I particularly appreciate the special assistance of Jean Atcheson, and Eileen Nadelson.

My resounding gratitude goes to my literary agent, Don Congdon, who, with great reassurance, has followed the development of this book.

To my wife, Lova, who endured and encouraged me until this book was completed, I give my deepest love and thanks.

It gives me great satisfaction to donate all sources and information I have collected about the case of Jack the Ripper to the Butler Library of Rare Books and Manuscripts, Columbia University, New York City. This collection can henceforth be used only for scientific purposes, under the supervision of Kenneth Lohf, Librarian, and Michael Sovern, President of Columbia University, or their authorized successors.

Introduction

DURING THE AUTUMN of 1888 in the grim slums of White-chapel in East London, five prostitutes were brutally murdered and mutilated. The murderer—who was never found—called himself Jack the Ripper; the mysterious name took hold of the public's imagination in a way that has never been equaled.

It was as a boy in Trondheim, Norway, where I was born, that I first heard of the appalling murders and of the sinister, yet jolly nickname given to the man who committed them. A philosophy student whom I knew had just returned from London, where she had visited Whitechapel. She told how Jack the Ripper almost magically disappeared into the anonymous darkness of the London streets. Though it was years since the murders had taken place, people were still haunted by his specter. I remember being shocked that the murderer had never been brought to justice.

As time went by, Jack the Ripper reached a special place in the romantic mythology of crime. I began to realize that his relationship to the world was never really decoded.

Two compelling mysteries have surrounded the case from the very beginning. Who was Jack the Ripper? And what were the forces that drove him to his savage murders? Many books have been written about his enigmatic identity, most of them making a claim for one candidate or another. But all these books are psychologically undernourished, because they have not addressed the second—and central—question. What was the motivation for these extraordinary crimes, crimes so brutal, yet so adeptly orchestrated?

As my career in medicine developed, I turned toward psychoanalysis and the psychiatry of crime. My interest in the Ripper murders increased and I constantly tried to keep abreast of any new or unusual item that surfaced on the case. I was astounded by the mounds of literature written on the Machiavellian subject and, at the same time, perplexed by the paucity of actual facts.

In 1981, when I was winding up my book about serial murderer David Berkowitz, "Son of Sam," I was invited to present a paper on the topic of serial murderers at the XIIth International Congress of the Academy of Forensic and Social Medicine in Vienna. My lecture, which appeared in the organization's May, 1982 issue, compared the Ripper murders with those of Son of Sam.

The enthusiastic reaction to my analogy was both appreciated and a bit surprising. But, when I reflected that I had addressed a European audience, people from the same environment where Jack the Ripper had played such havoc, I understood their strong interest. The similarities and differences between the two cases were so striking and the avenues of analysis so multifarious and inviting that I was persuaded to give the Ripper a more fully developed examination.

This will be the first time that a clinical and forensic psychiatrist and psychoanalyst has investigated and researched the one-hundred-year-old case of Jack the Ripper. A major drawback, of course, is that the suspects and the participating investigators have long since died.

The long-standing premise is that the case of Jack the Ripper is not provable. My deductions, however, are based on facts from sources that may be considered reliable. You will see that my findings speak for themselves and that my solution of the case is credible.

I was able to collect a great deal of new material concerning the crimes from medical books, treatises, and biological, psychological, pathological and sociological journals, as well as from medical doctors, libraries in England and the United States, and the records of a mental hospital where one of the suspects was confined and in which he died.

During this long and arduous search, I also retrieved the files on the tribe of humanity. It rends the web of shared values by which our community survives. Learning to stifle the criminal psyche is still very far off. But, unless we attempt to understand murderers, we partake to a certain extent in their darkness. As we uncover the emotional realities of crime, we are better able to see the dark side of our behavior and at the same time to help restore and heal the human spirit.

David Abrahamsen

PART ONE

THE EVIL WORLD OF WHITECHAPEL

POLICE NOTICE.

TO THE OCCUPIER.

On the mornings of Friday, 31st August, Saturday 8th, and Sunday, 30th September, 1888, Women were murdered in or near Whitechapel, supposed by some one residing in the immediate neighbourhood. Should you know of any person to whom suspicion is attached, you are earnestly requested to communicate at once with the nearest Police Station.

Metropolitan Police Office,
30th September, 1888.

Printed by M'Corquodale & Co. Limited, "The Armoury" Southwark

CHAPTER ONE

Victims in the Night

"With life so precarious, and opportunity for the happiness of life so remote, it is inevitable that life shall be cheap . . ."

JACK LONDON,
The People of the Abyss

T HE MURDERS AND mutilations of five prostitutes in White-chapel, in the East End of London, began on the morning of Friday, August 31, 1888. Mary Anne Nichols was found dead, lying in a back street named Buck's Row. Murders connected to theft or rape were common occurrences, and under ordinary circumstances the death of a prostitute would cause no more than a momentary ripple in the dark pool that was the East End. But these circumstances were not ordinary.

First of all, the motive was clearly not robbery, since Nichols had nothing to steal. Second, the violence of her death was chilling. Her throat was severed almost to the vertebrae. Her face was bruised, and both her upper and lower jaws were injured. A deep slash ran across her abdomen. The cuts had ragged edges and some inner organs had been cut out. The murder seemed to have no purpose except as an expression of violence. The police surgeon duly noted the details in his formal report to the London Metropolitan Police.

As an isolated event, the death of Nichols soon subsided in the public consciousness. After all, the Whitechapel of those days was one of the grimmest of all London slums; life there, as Jack London points out, was cheap indeed. One inhabitant of the East End wrote to *The Times* (London) at midcentury:

> We are Sur, as it may be, livin in a Wilderness, so far as the rest of London knows anything of us, or as the rich and great people care about. We live in muck and filthe. We aint got no privies, no dust bins, no drains, no water splies . . . We al of us suffer, and numbers are ill, and if the colera comes Lord help us . . .[1]

The writer accurately perceived that the place where he lived was so cut off from the rest of the prospering city that it was almost another country. The East End was the popular name for the area east of the actual City of London, which had grown up around the docks that lined the Thames, the heart of the trade on which the British Empire flourished. Inside this maze of narrow streets and jerry-built houses with totally inadequate sanitary facilities, some ninety thousand people lived in desperate poverty, victims of unemployment, homelessness, overcrowding and disease. The cholera did indeed come, and much worse. High infant mortality was as common as child labor, and prostitution, alcoholism, crime and murder were endemic. Hanging like an evil cloud over the slums was the thick black tarry smoke from factory smokestacks and thousands of coal fires that Charles Dickens describes at the beginning of *Bleak House*: "Smoke lowering down from chimney-pots, making a soft black drizzle, with flakes of soot in it as big as full-grown snow-flakes—gone into mourning, one might imagine, for the death of the sun."[2]

In *The People of the Abyss*—written a little over a decade after the infamous year of 1888—Jack London points out that the personal despair of many East Enders drove them to suicide.

Into this wilderness of poverty, illness and blight some Londoners traveled regularly to buy what could not be bought on more civilized streets—the sexual services of women. In the borough of Whitechapel alone there were ninety thousand people, of whom seventy thousand were women and children, mostly the unemployed poor who lived from hand to mouth. By 1880, there were estimated to be ten thousand prostitutes and three thousand brothels in London. Almost every room, nook or corridor in Whitechapel, Shadwell, Spitalfields and adjoining areas was at one time or another used for sexual purposes. Owning a brothel, in fact, was a favored way of investing in a neighborhood. Prostitution was illegal, of course, and many prostitutes were picked up and sent to jail. Men, however, were not harassed, unless they were suspected of performing "unnatural sexual acts" with other men. But the typical English method of dealing with the problem was, in general, to ignore its existence.

The most humane contemporary view of prostitution is found in the writings of the physician William Acton, one of the authors of the Contagious Diseases Act of 1866, which provided that prostitutes in certain areas be subject to periodic medical examination. In his pioneering book on the subject, first published in 1862, Acton writes that "cruel, biting poverty" forces women to become prostitutes:

Unable to obtain by their labor the means of procuring the bare necessaries of life, they gain, by surrendering their bodies to evil uses, food to sustain and clothes to cover them. Many thousand young women in the metropolis are unable by drudgery that lasts from early morning till late into the night to earn more than from 3s. to 5s. weekly. Many have to eke out their living as best they may on a miserable pittance for less than the least of the sums above-mentioned . . . Urged on by want and toil, encouraged by evil advisors, and exposed to selfish tempters, a large proportion of these girls fall from the path of virtue . . .[3]

The horror and sadness of the Jack the Ripper murders are intensified when we consider the degraded lives of the victims.

The Haymarket at midnight, where the gentry selected their pick of the night.

Scorned by society, these women were defenseless, alienated and dispossessed. Their lives were narrowly limited to the goal of getting four pence from a client to buy a shot of gin or a glass of beer, or to rent a bed for the night in a common lodging house. This economic exchange could easily end in syphilis or gonorrhea, or in an unwanted pregnancy that was terminated by an abortion performed under appalling conditions. Life, as they knew it, was dangerous and callous. In the "brute vulgarities" of this world, as Jack London put it, "the bad corrupts the good, and all fester together."[4]

Yet there were some people who felt that the prostitutes' deaths were a kind of moral retribution for the lives they led—essentially, that they got what they deserved. Syphilis was widely regarded as a punishment for sin—why not murder? Hypocrisy, one of the most deadly sins, was nowhere more evident in Victorian society than in the sexual double standard practiced by men. A woman was judged by her effect on men. This was a period when women of

6

one's own class were set on a pedestal and the wife was idealized as the keeper of the sacred flame of home and hearth: kind, gentle, nurturing and, above all, pure. And, not surprisingly, this produced a view of women as either virgins or whores. Although Victorian men publicly revered women, courted them, catered to them and married them, they secretly sought out prostitutes for sexual release or for taboo sexual pleasures. But there were other, psychological reasons why the Victorian man sought out prostitutes.

First of all, when a man bought the services of a prostitute, he did not have to establish any emotional relationship with her, or any significant relationship at all. The encounter was generally brief and impersonal. He did not have—and usually did not want—to remember her name or face.

A second reason was the great gulf of class distinction: almost without exception, prostitutes came from the lower classes. Their humble origins and the conditions of squalor in which they lived both excited and revolted the middle-class and aristocratic men who were their patrons. Slumming has always had charms for those who are not condemned to live in poverty, and many Victorian men visited the East End for very different reasons from their wives, who knew it only as a place to set up missions and soup kitchens to save souls and nourish starved bodies.

On the whole there is a general behavior pattern observable among those men who choose prostitutes as their only sexual objects. Such a man is unconsciously attracted to women who are more or less sexually discredited. He identifies with the harlot's lack of fidelity and loyalty. His choice is rooted in his unconscious fixation on his infantile feelings of tenderness for his mother, a crucial point in his sexual development. From his first belief that his mother is sexually pure, he comes to learn that she (like a prostitute) has had sex with a man (his father). The child feels betrayed by her. He fantasizes rescuing her from the father who he feels has defiled her. This leads him later in life to set up a woman

7

as a substitute mother whom he loves, yet despises for her weakness. He ends up seeking out prostitutes, whom he endows with his mother's image.

What drives women to prostitution? Without question, it is a way of obtaining through economic means what a woman has not been able to gain through love, the love from a mother or father, or a substitute. For some women, prostitution seems to offer a means of revenging themselves against weak and passive fathers who never defended them against their mothers' anger and criticism. Other women feel a masochistic identification of sex as sinful or humiliating, as they believe it was for their own mothers. In nineteenth-century Whitechapel, the wretched housing, miserable earnings and lack of emotional bonds between parents and children inevitably produced strained and callous relationships. Girls moved away from their parents into a situation where the procurer, the pimp, became the father substitute and the madam the mother substitute. The girl's relationship with her abusing father and unloving mother was now played out in the new environment, complete with all the former ambivalent feelings. One must wonder why a woman abused by her mother would become a prostitute and tolerate the madam. The answer is that she hates the madam as she hated her mother, yet is masochistically tied to her.

For most of the Whitechapel prostitutes, their illicit business was a means of scraping by from day to day in a poverty-stricken world. It had desperate and cruel consequences—broken homes and emotional turmoil, sometimes leading to arrest and jail, in addition to the risk of disease, alcoholism, drug addiction and exposure to crime. Even if a prostitute married or managed to avoid the fate of poverty and disease, her psychological fate remained cloudy at best.

The eternal wish of every woman from childhood onward is to be taken care of by someone who loves her. But few are given such happiness. And the prostitutes of Whitechapel were no exception. For five of them, a horrible death ended their quest.

Falling from the path of virtue had always been dangerous; the story of Mary Anne Nichols shows that it was becoming more so.

Nichols was no young girl, however; she was forty-two years old and an alcoholic. She had had five children and had left her husband about eight years earlier because of her drinking habits. Though separated from her, her husband continued to support her for several years until she moved in with another man. Several times, Nichols had tried to make a fresh start, but her alcoholism always prevailed. At one point she ended up in a workhouse, but was thrown out because she stole some small items—again, the result of her drinking. *The Times* (London) described her life as "intemperate, irregular and vicious."[5] The meaning of "vicious" here is "savage."

On the night of August 30, 1888, Nichols had been drinking steadily at a pub. At about 2:00 A.M., she decided to go out on the streets to raise the price of a bed for the night. She went into Buck's Row, a secluded back alley about a hundred yards from the Jews' Cemetery, close to the Whitechapel Road. At about 3:45 A.M., her body was discovered there by Constable John Neil working his Whitechapel beat. *The Times* (London) described Neil's discovery of the body:

> With the aid of his lamp he examined the body and saw blood oozing from a wound in the throat. Deceased was lying on her back with her clothes disarranged. [Neil] felt her arm, which was quite warm from the joints upward, while her eyes were wide open.[6]

She was dressed in a new brown dress, a shabby red overcoat, two flannel petticoats, blue woolen stockings and a straw bonnet, which had fallen from her head and was lying by her side. Her underwear had been removed. Her only possessions were a piece of mirror, a comb and a handkerchief.

The police surgeon Henry Llewellyn of 152 Whitechapel Road was called to the scene and examined the body at the site. He found no marks of a struggle and no bloody trail as if the body had been dragged. He had the body moved to the mortuary, where he discovered for the first time the mutilation of the abdomen. He concluded that the cuts must have been caused by a moderately sharp, long-bladed knife wielded with violence. Excerpts from his report to the Metropolitan Police the following day, August 31, 1888, are as follows:

> . . . throat cut nearly severing head from body, abdomen cut open from centre of bottom of ribs along right side, under pelvis to left of stomach, there the wound was jagged: the coating of the stomach was cut in several places and two small stabs on private parts . . .[7]

Inquiries were made of the neighbors, night watchmen, other prostitutes and friends of Nichols, local tavern owners, coffee-stall keepers and lodging houses. The police also interrogated three slaughtermen doing night work for a butcher's firm on the next street, but each accounted for himself satisfactorily. Nichols's history "did not disclose the slightest pretext for a motive on the part of her friends or associates in the common lodging houses," wrote Chief Inspector Donald S. Swanson in his report on the murder.[8]

Early on Saturday, September 8, 1888, London was jolted once again, when the body of another murdered woman was found. Forty-seven-year-old Annie Chapman—also destitute, a prostitute and an alcoholic—was discovered in the back yard of a house on Hanbury Street, Spitalfields, about half a mile from the site of Nichols's murder. This woman had also been hideously mutilated. It was suggested "that the murderer, for some purpose or other, whether from a morbid motive or for the sake of gain, had committed the crime for the purpose of possessing himself of the uterus."[9]

The scene was macabre. Fully dressed, she lay on the ground with her organs exposed like a scientific experiment. The abdominal wall had been cut open and the uterus removed. The vagina, bladder and intestines—still attached to the body—were arranged over her right shoulder. At her feet were her comb and some coins, carefully placed.

On Friday, September 14, 1888, *The Times* (London) described the postmortem of Annie Chapman and stated that, in the coroner's opinion, "there had been no struggle between the murderer and the woman." This was an important finding. Like Nichols, Chapman had died without making any resistance. The coroner also concluded that the murderer "had anatomical knowledge from the way the viscera was removed." In addition, he believed the murder weapon was not an ordinary knife, but "a small amputating knife or a well-ground slaughterman's knife," probably between six and eight inches long. [10]

Annie Chapman was the widow of a veterinarian. They had been separated for several years before his death because of what the police report called "her drunken and immoral ways." However, her husband continued to send her ten shillings a week until he died, at Christmas, 1886. Like Nichols, Chapman was a victim of her alcoholism, which had caused her to lose touch with her family and turn to prostitution. *The Times* (London) on September 27, 1888, reported:

> She had evidently lived an immoral life for some time, and her habits and surroundings had become worse since her means had failed. She no longer visited her relations, and her brother had not seen her for five months, when she borrowed a small sum from him. She lived principally in the common lodging houses in the neighborhood of Spitalfields, where such as she were herded like cattle. She showed signs of great deprivation, as if she had been badly fed.
>
> The glimpse of life in those dens which the evidence in this case disclosed was sufficient to make them feel there was much in the 19th-century civilization of which they had small reason to be proud . . . [11]

On Saturday, September 15, 1888, *The Lancet*, the foremost British medical journal, published an editorial suggesting the theory that the murderer might be a lunatic. But, the writer added, this "appears to us to be by no means at present well established."[12]

The third victim was Elizabeth Stride, forty-five years old, a Swedish prostitute known by the name of "Long Liz." On Sunday, September 30, her body was found at Berner Street, Aldgate, a short distance from Hanbury Street. Although her throat had been cut in the now familiar method, she had not been disemboweled, which suggested that the murderer was interrupted in his work. Did somebody warn him?

Later that same night, the murderer struck again, at Mitre Square, which was only about half a mile from Berner Street, just across the boundary of the City of London. The victim was another prostitute, Catherine Eddowes, who was forty-three. As if in compensation for the murderer's frustration at having had to leave Stride intact, Eddowes's body had been brutally dissected. Her nose was cut off, her abdomen sliced open, and on her right shoulder were placed her left kidney and intestines.

The fact that this murder took place within the City boundaries meant that it was handled by the City Police Department, and these fresh investigators zealously set about gathering evidence. Eddowes's murder, it seems, was the only occasion when a description of the possible assailant was available.

Catherine Eddowes had been trying to make some extra money by picking hops in Kent with her friend, John Kelly, who had spent 2s. 6d. of his earnings to buy her a pair of boots. When they returned to London together on Thursday, September 27, however, they had to pawn the boots to get enough money to pay for a night's lodging. The following night they had to part and she spent the night in the Mile End casual ward (a dormitory), while Kelly stayed in a cheap lodging house. By Saturday they had no money left and were unable to find any odd jobs. So at 2:00 P.M., Eddowes left Kelly and went off to Bermondsey to try to borrow money from her daughter. At 8:00 P.M. that evening, she was back in the City, in a drunk and disorderly condition, was arrested by two City policemen and taken to the Bishopsgate Police Station, where she remained until shortly after midnight. During her incarceration, she continued, in the words of Dr. Francis Camps, one of the major authorities on the Ripper story, "singing to herself and asking to be released." His report continued:

> At about 1 A.M. her wish was complied with and she was shooed off into the night. It was a singularly bad piece of luck for her that the instructions of Major Smith, the City Police Commissioner, were not carried out, for he had ordered that every man and woman seen together after midnight must be accounted for and she might have been followed to Mitre Square. [13]

As City Police Commissioner, Major Smith was responsible for all police activity within the City of London, while the Metropolitan Police were under the separate command of General Sir Charles Warren, who had no jurisdiction within the City. Both commanders were out in the field that night, and Smith, a more enthusiastic participant than Warren, was intensely frustrated to discover later on that he had been on the heels of the murderer the whole time.

It was a City constable, P. C. Watkins, who found Catherine Eddowes's body. He had passed through the square at 1:30 A.M. and noticed nothing unusual, but when he returned, about fifteen minutes later, his police lantern at once illuminated the body of a woman lying on her back in the corner of the square with her left leg extended and her right leg bent at the knee. Further investigation showed the shocking nature of her wounds, which were subsequently noted by the police surgeon in some pencil drawings made at the scene.

Subsequently, it seemed, the murderer had made his way from Mitre Square across Houndsditch and Middlesex Street to Goulston Street, where a blood-stained rag from Eddowes's apron was found at 2:55 A.M. To confuse the public and the police still more, a chalked message about the Jews—"The Jewes are not the men that will be blamed for nothing"—was found in the passageway at Goulston Street. Neither the rag nor the message had been there half an hour before when the police constable passed through on his beat at 2:20 A.M.

As soon as Major Smith was told of this discovery, he dispatched an inspector with two detectives to photograph the message, but General Warren had arrived in Goulston Street meanwhile and took it upon himself to order the writing rubbed out at once, without waiting for the photographer, on the grounds that he feared it would incite an anti-Jewish riot. We shall hear more later about this mysterious communication about the "Jewes."

While the police doctors, F. G. Brown and George Sequiera, were examining the body in Mitre Square, the murderer apparently left Goulston Street and went north to Dorset Street, where he paused to wash blood off his hands at a public sink. This suggested that he knew the neighborhood, because the sink was set back from the street. Passersby observed the blood shortly afterward.

Eddowes's body was removed to the mortuary. It was stripped and an autopsy carried out, but the body was not identified until Tuesday, October 2, by her friend John Kelly. Ironically, his last words to Eddowes had been a warning to her to be careful of the Ripper; he had been lulled into a false sense of security by the fact that one of his friends had seen her being taken to the police station. It was he who identified her shattered body, finally, by the pawn ticket found in her bonnet for the boots he himself had bought a few days earlier. (Her own husband took two weeks to come forward, having changed his name to avoid being traced by her.)

At the Eddowes inquest in October 1888, a commercial traveler named Joseph Lawende and a J. H. Levy reported having seen a man and a woman talking together at the corner of the court leading to Mitre Square in Duke Street shortly before the murder.

Nov 11 th

A 4930 1/205

16   C

Plan for entrapping the Whitechapel murderer.

Let a number of men —, say twelve be selected, of short stature, and as far as possible of effeminate appearance, but of known courage & tried nerve. Dress them as females if this class from whom this murderer has selected, Arm them with the best and lightest weapons

and cloth both them over the district haunted by the murderer.

—¦—

Note, the men would again to be fair actors, and behave in the natural manner of that class further they would require to be —

— they would require to be Shadowed by help's, in an unobtrusive way, and the whole scheme would require to be kept absolutely secret, for once let this become get a hint of it, and farewell

to any chance of success.

This plan is based on the theory that the murderer neither solicits interviews and that the woman accompanys him to a quiet spot, where the crime is committed, while in the act committed, so that men who undertake the duty of capturing him would require to farewell their wits about them.

Tho Blair
Gritton
Dumfries
NB.

One of the many letters to London police offering tactics to ensnare the Ripper. (Home Office Records, November 11, 1888)

The police released the following description: "Thirty years old, five feet nine inches in height, with a small fair moustache, dressed in something like navy serge and with a deerstalker's hat, peak fore and after. He also wore a red handkerchief."[14]

Until 1966, this was the only description given of a man seen close to the scene of the murder. My own research has turned up other and more substantial findings.

By now the whole of London was in an uproar. Suggestions for catching the murderer poured in from all quarters. A Mr. Blair wrote from Dumfries to suggest the use of decoys:

> Let a number of men—say twelve—be selected, of short stature, and as far as possible of effeminate appearance, but of known courage & tried nerve, dress them as females of the class from whom the victims are selected, arm them with the best and lightest weapons and distribute them over the district haunted by the murderer.
>
> Note, The men would require to be fair actors, and behave in the natural manner of women of that class, further they would require to be shadowed by help, in an unobtrusive way, and the whole scheme would require to be kept absolutely secret, for once let the press get a hint of it, and farewell to any chance of success.[15]

Mr. Blair added that his plan was "based on the theory that the murderer solicits intercourse, and that the woman accompanies him to a quiet spot, where the crime is committed while in the act, so that men who undertook the duty of capturing him would require to have all their wits about them."[16]

A civil servant with the Customs Department became convinced that the murders were the work of Portuguese sailors, because, he said, they had contracted venereal disease from a prostitute and were acting out the "characteristic revengefulness of the Portuguese race." His theory was carefully, if illogically, set forth and Scotland Yard treated it seriously for a while, then concluded the man was "a troublesome faddist."[17]

An engraver wrote to the Yard suggesting that a full pardon be offered to the murderer and that, when he turned himself in, the promise should be ignored: "for once [we should] break our national word of honour for the benefit of the universe."[18]

The fact that the murderer had shown some skill in eviscerating the bodies led the police to suppose that the Ripper might have a medical background, and the police spent much time tracking down "three insane medical students." The police also employed bloodhounds, though to little effect. In the Scotland Yard files I also found a "Secret" memorandum ordering a supply of tricycles for the police to enable them to follow more quickly on the trail of the mysterious assassin who struck with such lightning speed. Local Whitechapel businessmen formed a Vigilance Committee, headed by Mr. George Lusk.[19] A Member of Parliament named Samuel Montagu suggested that a reward be paid for the murderer's capture.[20] Terrified prostitutes continued to ply their trade, however; they had no other means of support.

For forty days following Eddowes's death, nothing happened. It seemed that, temporarily, the violent homicidal impulses of the murderer had become satiated. But on Friday, November 9, a twenty-five-year-old prostitute named Marie Jeanette Kelly was found dead at Miller's Court, Spitalfields, in the vicinity of Hanbury Street. This murder took place in the privacy of Kelly's own room in Miller's Court, and not in the streets. The murderer, therefore, had the safety and leisure to commit the bloodiest butchery of them all.

London policemen who saw Kelly's body never forgot it. She was unrecognizable. Her skin was flayed on the face, upper body and thighs, and the flesh removed on some parts so that only her skeleton remained. The bed and night table had bits of flesh on them. Her nose and ears were cut off and her liver was located at her feet. Her uterus was mutilated. Her amputated breasts and kidneys were carefully placed on a nearby table. A doctor who had viewed the body reported to an American newspaper that the sight of the murdered woman surpassed all his gory experiences.

Once again, those who examined the victim concluded that the murder knife was wielded with some knowledge and practice. At the autopsy it was discovered that Kelly was pregnant.

The Metropolitan Police and Scotland Yard continued their massive investigations, and millions of Londoners became hostages to the night as they waited for Jack the Ripper to be caught. It was a name he had introduced for himself in one of his cocky notes to the authorities and it immediately captured the public's imagination. Everybody had an idea about the identity of the murderer, and it seemed that almost everybody passed on their suggestions to Scotland Yard, which painstakingly investigated each one they thought worthy and filed the others away.

In a memo on October 25, 1888, a police report to the Home Office noted:

> That a crime of this kind should have been committed without any clue being supplied by the criminal is unusual, but that four successive murders should have been committed without our having the slightest clue of any kind is extraordinary, if not unique, in the annals of crime.
>
> The result has been to necessitate our giving attention to innumerable suggestions, such as would in any ordinary case be dismissed unnoticed, and no hint of any kind, which was not obviously absurd, has been neglected. Moreover, the activity of the Police has been to a considerable extent wasted through the exigencies of sensational journalism, and the action of unprincipled persons, who, from various motives, have endeavoured to mislead us.[21]

The Ripper murders stopped just as suddenly as they had started. It was some months before it became apparent that the nightmare was over, but like everything about the case, it was a puzzle to know why. Had the murderer become insane, or fled the country, or had he himself died or been murdered? The guesses were as diverse as the list of people whom the police interrogated about the murders, or on whom public suspicion rested, however briefly.

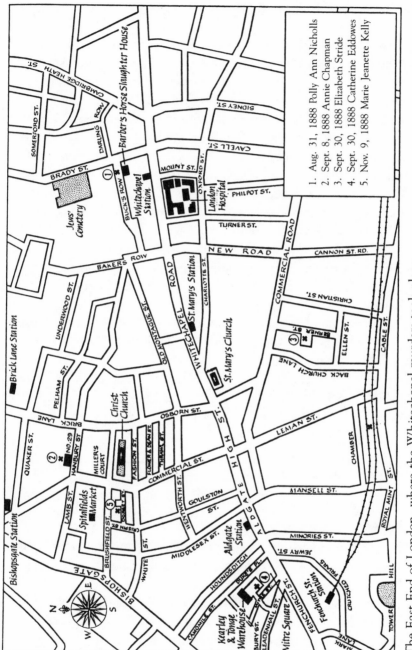

The following legend appears on the map:

1. Aug. 31, 1888 Polly Ann Nicholls
2. Sept. 8, 1888 Annie Chapman
3. Sept. 30, 1888 Elizabeth Stride
4. Sept. 30, 1888 Catherine Eddowes
5. Nov. 9, 1888 Marie Jeanette Kelly

The East End of London, where the Whitechapel murders took place.

Whatever the reason, there were no more murders following Kelly's death that bore the Ripper's bloody and unmistakable trademarks. And despite the days and months of dogged work by the police, the case remained unsolved. Eventually, the official files and a mass of papers connected with them passed into the archives of Scotland and New Scotland Yard, some marked with the top confidential notation: "closed until 1993."[22] Despite the British practice not to publish information about a controversial event for at least a century, I obtained permission to release the material in this book. The Jack the Ripper murders became a part of history.

There has always been some dispute about how many women Jack the Ripper killed; the number has varied from five to twelve. But the common features in the five murders presented here, I believe, are conclusive.

All five murders shared certain characteristics. They all took place in an area within one square mile of each other. All were committed between the hours of eleven at night and five in the morning. Each took place on a weekend. The throat of each victim had been severed, and with the exception of Stride, the body carved up and mutilated with a knife. And all of their faces were congested. An article in *The Lancet* which described the circumstances of one of the murders "suggests that the absence of a cry was due to strangulation being the real cause of death, a common practice of sexual murders."[23]

All the women were prostitutes, suggesting a psychologically intimate, if unconscious, connection between the murderer and his victims. They were destitute, vulnerable and alcoholic. Four out of the five were over forty years old and had borne children. Kelly was pregnant.

The mystery of Jack the Ripper's identity is a major reason for the persistence of the myth. Considering the vast efforts of both police and public, even in those days when investigation was a much more primitive business, it is remarkable that he was never apprehended.

The grotesque murders instilled widespread terror not only throughout London itself, but also across a nation that was already gripped by strong anti-Jewish feelings and fears of radical movements that would lead to political anarchy. Faced with confusion and incredulity over the murders, the police were involved simultaneously in trying to pursue the investigations, reassure frightened citizens, and prevent future attacks.

A divided leadership within the police department exacerbated their difficulties. Individual policemen who remained diligent in their duties were nonetheless hampered in their activities. But weak leadership within the police was far from being the only catalyst of an explosion of social unrest. On the flip side of police ineptitude lay its power structure designed to protect the upper strata of England's monarchy.

In 1886, two years before the Whitechapel murders, bloody riots and demonstrations had erupted in Pall Mall and Oxford Street. Fueled by continuing mass unemployment, the upheavals continued into the following year, with unemployed workers camping out in the parks and Trafalgar Square on a semi-permanent basis. Finally, a confrontation took place on November 13, 1887, in Trafalgar Square between a huge mob of demonstrators and several thousand men from the Metropolitan Police; inevitably, there were injuries and massive arrests, and the day became known as "Bloody Sunday."

The Home Secretary appointed General Charles Warren, a professional soldier, as Chief Commissioner of the Metropolitan Police, and it was Warren who handled the confrontation in Trafalgar Square. His success in controlling the riots was rewarded with a knighthood, but his harsh tactics increased public outcry and agitation. Renewed outbursts of dissatisfaction with Warren surfaced during the investigation of the Whitechapel murders.

Warren was not only taken to task for the failure of his men to find the Ripper, but he was also rumored to be a Freemason.[24] In today's society, Freemasonry is considered perfectly respectable, but at that time Freemasons were thought to be potential anar-

21

chists because they operated under a clandestine code. It has been subsequently suggested that the rumors themselves were a diversionary tactic masking the involvement in the Whitechapel murders of certain powerful men in the government, and even in the royal family.

There were reasons for Warren's inept handling of the murders. In the first place, he was deprived of full authority to conduct the investigations. Although he had been brought in originally to reorganize the police force, the Metropolitan Police continued to operate under dual supervision. The General was given control only of the operations of the uniformed branch, while the Criminal Investigations Department (CID) remained under the command of a superintendent who dealt directly with the Home Office.[25]

There is considerable mystery as to the extent of Warren's responsibility for the investigation of the Ripper murders. He certainly paid an almost instant visit to the passageway at Goulston Street where the mysterious message had been chalked on the wall: "The Jewes are not the men that will be blamed for nothing."[26]

The inspector in charge of the case appealed to Warren to know what action he should take; Warren told him to erase the message immediately, without waiting for the photographer summoned by Major Smith of the City Police, who was expected within the hour. Warren claimed that the reason for the erasure was to prevent an anti-Jewish riot, and his report to the Home Secretary of November 6, 1888, consists of a lengthy defense of this position:

4 Whitehall Place, S.W.
6th November 1888

Confidential
The Under Secretary of State
The Home Office

Sir,

In reply to your letter of the 5th instant, I enclose a report of the circumstances of the Mitre Square Murder so far as they have come under the notice of the Metropolitan Police, and I now give an account regarding the erasing the writing on the wall in Goulston Street which I have already partially explained to Mr. Matthews verbally.

On the 30th September on hearing of the Berner Street murder, after visiting Commercial Street Station I arrived at Leman Street Station shortly before 5 A.M. and ascertained from Superintendent Arnold all that was known there relative to the two murders.

The most pressing question at that moment was some writing on the wall in Goulston Street evidently written with the intention of inflaming the public mind against the Jews, and which Mr. Arnold with a view to prevent serious disorder proposed to obliterate, and had sent down an Inspector with a sponge for that purpose, telling him to await his arrival.

I considered it desirable that I should decide this matter myself, as it was one involving so great a responsibility whether any action was taken or not.

I accordingly went down to Goulston Street at once before going to the scene of the murder: it was just getting light, the public would be in the streets in a few minutes, in a neighbourhood very much crowded on Sunday mornings by Jewish vendors and Christian purchasers from all parts of London.

There were several Police around the spot when I arrived, both Metropolitan and City.

The writing was on the jamb of the open archway or doorway visible to anybody *in the street* and could not be covered up without danger of the covering being torn off at once.

23

A discussion took place whether the writing could *be left covered up* or otherwise or whether any portion of it could be left for an hour until it could be photographed; but after taking into consideration the excited state of the population in London generally at the time, the strong feeling which had been excited against the Jews, and the fact that in a short time there would be a large concourse of the people in the streets, and having before me the Report that if it was left there the house was likely to be wrecked (in which from my own observation I entirely concurred) I considered it desirable to obliterate the writing at once, having taken a copy of which I enclose a duplicate.

After having been to the scene of the murder, I went on to the City Police Office and informed the Chief Superintendent of the reason why the writing had been obliterated.

I may mention that so great was the feeling with regard to the Jews that on the 13th ulto. the Acting Chief Rabbi wrote to me on the subject of the spelling of the word "Jewes" on account of a newspaper asserting that this was Jewish spelling in the Yiddish dialect. He added "in the present state of excitement it is dangerous to the safety of the poor Jews in the East [End] to allow such an assertion to remain uncontradicted. My community keenly appreciates your humane and vigilant action during this critical time."

It may be realised therefore if the safety of the Jews in Whitechapel could be considered to be jeopardised 13 days after the murder by the question of the spelling of the word Jews, what might have happened to the Jews in that quarter had that writing been left intact.

I do not hesitate myself to say that if that writing had been left there would have been an onslaught upon the Jews, property would have been wrecked, and lives would probably have been lost; and I was much gratified with the promptitude with which Superintendent Arnold was prepared to act in the matter if I had not been there.

I have no doubt myself whatever that one of the principal objects of the Reward offered by Mr. Montagu was to shew to the world that the Jews were desirous of having the Hanbury Street Murder cleared up, and thus to divert from them the very strong feeling which was then growing up.

I am, Sir,

> Your most obedient Servant,
> (signed) C. Warren[27]

Warren enclosed two identical copies of the following message:

> The Jewes are
> The men that
> Will not
> be Blamed
> for nothing[28]

There has been some argument about whether the spelling was "Jewes" or "Juwes," the exact position of the word "not" (which differs in the version above from that given earlier), and whether there was significance in the breaks in the message. But it seems clear that the purpose of the message was diabolically cunning—the Ripper intended to throw the police off the scent, linking the message to the murder through the rag from Eddowes's apron; no doubt he also disliked the Jews, and he may well have hoped to incite the sort of anti-Jewish demonstration Warren's swift decision prevented.

In fact, several chief suspects in the murders were Jewish. One, a Polish Jew named John Pizer, was known to be a small-time blackmailer and abuser of prostitutes. He was a boot finisher by trade, and when the police came to question him they found several sharp knives and a leather apron on the premises. Since a leather apron had been found not far from the body of Annie Chapman, he was taken to the police station and jailed on suspicion of her murder. However, the apron turned out to belong to a neighbor on Hanbury Street. Pizer's alibi held up, and the police were forced to release him.

The Jews were particularly unpopular in Whitechapel, where they formed a considerable proportion of the population, and the situation had not been helped by a notorious murder case, some four years earlier, when a Jew named Lipski had been hanged for the murder of his Jewish girlfriend.

Sir Charles Warren considered social liberation in England a critical issue. The Britain of this era was great indeed, rich and authoritative, proud possessor of an Empire on which the sun never set, in which members of a burgeoning middle class could hope to reap rewards, too—although the mansions and great estates were still the privilege of the selected and wealthy few. The British fleet ruled the oceans.

The extravagant lifestyle of the rich was in stark contrast to that of the many slum dwellers who struggled in the wilderness of poverty, alcohol and illness. In general, members of the aristocratic class lived in an atmosphere of luxury and festivity and appeared to pass their days entirely in entertaining themselves. Very few participated in helping the more unfortunate or were prepared to take on genuine responsibilities. The royal family, in particular, was criticized. Queen Victoria lived almost entirely in retirement at Windsor, in the Highlands or on the Isle of Wight, while the Prince of Wales, denied by his mother any opportunity to participate in the business of ruling, spent most of his time hunting, going to parties, traveling around Europe or making triumphal trips through India. People observed, also, that though the Prince had married the beautiful and popular Alexandra, he regularly left her at home while he continued his peripatetic existence, constantly meeting with other attractive women. Such behavior earned him positive dislike in many quarters. His elder son Prince Albert Victor, known as Eddy, was a very unprepossessing heir to the throne and, as we shall hear later, involved in scandals. Even the Princess of Wales's personal popularity could not bring people to think well of her neglectful husband or look forward to Prince Eddy's ascent to the throne.

There were those who agreed with Warren on the social and class inequities. Nevertheless, the General began to feel outcast and isolated. Six months earlier, in March 1888, he had informed the Home Secretary of his intention to resign. The idea of a conspiracy directed by the Freemasons seems extremely questionable; more likely, there may have been some interference by various officials in the murder investigations, including cover-ups and glossing over of possible suspects. It was probably the personality more than the practices of Sir Charles Warren that created controversy and condemnation.

Earlier, Warren appointed as his assistant commissioner a man named Robert Anderson. There were several curious features about Anderson's involvement in the case. The new assistant had arranged to take a vacation in Switzerland and was to begin his duties on his return. The murder of Mary Anne Nichols in Buck's Row took place on August 31, eight days before Anderson was due to leave, and Annie Chapman was murdered on Hanbury Street on September 8, the morning of that eighth day. Despite these dual emergencies, however, Anderson refused to postpone his vacation and departed as planned. Barely a month later, Anderson seemed to be taking credit for the operation by submitting an updated report of the murder investigations to the Home Secretary's Office, though he had had very little to do with its preparation.

As if adding insult to injury, the Home Secretary's Office kept issuing orders directly to Anderson and Warren's other subordinates, rather than routing them through the General himself. This deliberate bypassing of the regular channels caused confusion and resentment throughout the police division and certainly slowed the investigation of the Whitechapel murders. A catch-22 situation evolved in which Warren was severely hampered in his efforts to capture Jack the Ripper while being criticized for not devoting his efforts to the capture of Jack the Ripper.

In the House of Commons on November 12, 1888, Mr. Conybeare rose to question the Home Secretary.

RESIGNATION OF SIR C. WARREN.

Mr. CONYBEARE asked the Secretary of State for the Home Department whether he could state the exact reason why the late head of the Detective Department in the Metropolitan Police resigned his position; whether it was the fact that Sir C. Warren had now practically the direct control of the Detective Department; and whether, in view of the constant recurrence of atrocious murders, and the failure of the new organisation and methods to detect the murderer, he would consider the propriety of making some change in the arrangements of Scotland-yard. The hon. member also wished to know whether it was true, as reported in the newspapers that afternoon, that Sir C. Warren had tendered his resignation, and that it had been accepted.

The HOME SECRETARY.—I have already more than once stated the reason why Mr. Monro resigned. With regard to the remainder of the question, Mr. Anderson is now in direct control of the Criminal Investigation Department, under the superintendence and control, as provided by statute, of the Chief Commissioner. The failure of the police, so far, to detect the person guilty of the Whitechapel murders is due, not to any new reorganisation in the department, but to the extraordinary cunning and secrecy which characterise the commission of the crimes. I have for some time had the question of the whole system of the Criminal Investigation Department under my consideration, with a view to introducing any improvement that may be required. With regard to the last question, I have to inform the hon. member that the Chief Commissioner of Police did on the 8th inst. tender his resignation to her Majesty's Government, and that his resignation has been accepted (loud Opposition cheers).[29]

Finding the continual erosion of his status intolerable, Warren had in fact tendered his resignation on November 8, and the Home Secretary now confirmed to Mr. Conybeare that it had been accepted, amid loud cheering from the political opposition.

Despite the bifurcated police operations, the CID (now being run by Anderson) fervently pursued all potential clues that might lead them to the murderer. They increased the number of police-men on the case and interrogated an ever-growing number of suspects.

Among those suspected were the seamen whose ships came to London, unloaded their cargo, then left and returned again on a fairly regular basis at the end of each week. The list of crew and cattlemen issued by the Statistical Department of the London Custom House on November 15, 1888, shows that every one of those examined at great length by the police proved to have a watertight alibi.

During their investigations, the department also discussed the idea of offering rewards to those who could help them in their inquiries, but in line with British morality, rewards were felt to be unnecessary, and Mr. Montagu's offer of five hundred pounds was never taken up.

Almost unanimously, the newspapers expressed the outrage of a British public held hostage by fear and panic. The only way of easing the tension was to find the murderer and bring him to justice.

1. *The Times* (London), circa 1850's.
2. Charles Dickens, *Bleak House*, Bradbury and Evan, London, 1853, p. 1.
3. William Acton, *Prostitution, Considered in its Moral, Social, and Sanitary Aspects, in London and other large cities and Garrison Towns, with Proposals for the Control and Prevention of its Attendant Evils*, John Churchill, London 1862, as quoted in Steven Marcus, *The Other Victorians; A Study of Sexuality and Pornography in Mid-Nineteenth-Century England*. Basic Books, New York [1966], p. 7.
4. Jack London, *The People of the Abyss*, Macmillan & Co., New York, 1903, p. 152.
5. *The Times* (London), September 1, 1888.
6. *Ibid.*

7. Report by Henry Llewellyn, Metropolitan Police, London, August 31, 1888.
8. Report by Chief Inspector Swanson, Metropolitan Police, London, September 2, 1888.
9. *The Lancet*, September 29, 1888, p. 637.
10. *The Times* (London), September 14, 1888.
11. *Ibid.*, September 27, 1888.
12. *The Lancet*, September 15, 1888, pp. 533–534.
13. Report by Professor Francis E. Camps, *London Hospital Gazette*, Vol. LXIX, No. 1, April, 1966.
14. *Coroner's Inquest: Catherine Eddowes*, No. 135, 1888.
15. Letter by Mr. Blair to Home Secretary, November 11, 1888.
16. *Ibid.*
17. Letter to Scotland Yard, October, 1888.
18. *Ibid.*
19. Memo to Mr. Lusk, Public Record Office, Scotland Yard, Oct 7, 1888.
20. *Daily Chronicle*, July 19, 1889.
21. London Police Report to Home Secretary, October 25, 1888.
22. Files of Whitechapel Murders, Public Record Office, Scotland Yard, July, 1892.
23. *The Lancet*, September 8, 1888.
24. *Ars Quatuor Coronatorum*, Transactions, Lodge No. 2076, Vol. 99, September, 1987, Adlaird & Son, The Garden City Press.
25. Geoffrey Trease, *London: A Concise History*, New York, 1975, p. 138.
26. Martin Howells & Keith Skinner, *The Ripper Legacy: The Life and Death of Jack the Ripper*, Sidgwick & Jackson, London, 1987, pp. 16–17.
27. Report by Charles Warren to Home Secretary, London, November 6, 1888.
28. *Ibid.*
29. *The Standard*, November 13, 1888.

CHAPTER TWO

The Murdering Mind

"Though this be madness, yet there is method in't."

WILLIAM SHAKESPEARE,
Hamlet II, ii

"I wanted to destroy her . . . a pretty girl, a threat to me, to my masculinity."

DAVID BERKOWITZ,
the "Son of Sam" in an
interview with the author on
May 17, 1979.

THE IMPULSE TO kill lies within us all. Every one of us is a repository of stormy, agitating and disturbing emotions that have grown out of our pasts. We have rages, frustrations and fantasies—even murderous ones. Most of us do not act on these fantasies. What differentiates the man who actually commits murder from those who merely fantasize such crimes?[1]

My answer comes from many years of research and psychoanalysis of the mind of murderers. A long and conspicuous list of mental and sexual disorders and aberrations unfolds in those who murder. Every one of the some fifty murderers I have examined had distorted sexual emotions with little or no male identification. Each led a rich and exaggerated fantasy life, exhibited hate and

31

anger directed at others as well as himself, and had a desire for revenge. Fear and depression oppressed them all. At the root of these characteristics lie intense feelings of frustration, insignificance, worthlessness and impotence. The murderer feels like a nobody—feels like killing himself.[2]

Between the victim and the murderer is an often unseen tie that is both emotional and sexual, because the sexual drive is intimately connected with murderous and hating emotions. In fact, I will go further: the sexual force often manifested as revenge, jealousy and envy is the power that mobilizes, stimulates and maintains the impulses to murder. Without such a sexual stimulus, there would be few pathological murders.

Because sexual emotions are practically always involved in homicide, it is safe to conclude that Jack the Ripper's sexual feelings played a significant role in his murderous activities. When we understand the intimate connection between sex and murder, we can recognize how closely intertwined are love and hate. A child, for example, may feel a passionate hate in direct proportion to the love—or need—he feels for someone. As a person matures normally, the extremes of love and hate become gradually balanced. But until that emotional maturity is attained, the sexual drive, expressed in loving feelings and actions, is profoundly associated with hateful feelings and actions. The person feeling the hate, however, may not be able to associate his emotions directly with his actions because such emotions are outside of his consciousness.

The mind of a murderer is charged with hateful or ambivalent feelings that have been stored in him since early childhood. When a child is hurt by rejection or criticism, he either gives vent to his distress or, as frequently happens, pushes the incident out of his mind. If he is unable to express himself, or if he forbids himself to have unfriendly, hostile feelings about anyone, especially parents or parent figures, then he must "forget" or repress the event. The resentment lingers on, however, stored in his unconscious mind. In maladjusted people, this resentment builds into anger or hate—like steam gathering in a pressure cooker. Repressed anger turns into anxiety, and anxiety is even more upsetting than anger. Years of anxiety mount and, in the murderer, become intolerable; acting out the fantasy becomes his only release.

Each of us has seen a thwarted child who impulsively throws a temper tantrum. His rage expresses his powerlessness; he isn't getting his way. The murderer is like this child. Early in life, he has been frustrated in getting what he wants—for example, his father's or his mother's love—or he has not been able to empower himself through the normal process of growing up and separating himself from his parents. Inside him seethe ancient reservoirs of powerlessness and dependency, ready to boil over. Powerlessness leads to frustration, then rage. Murder externalizes these explosive emotions.

At the root of powerlessness lies fear. In the case of men who murder women, it is a fear of women, and the fear is temporarily banished by the act of murder, just as the child gains temporary power through his temper tantrums. For a brief, intense, gratifying moment, the murderer has power over the woman who threatens him. He holds sway over life and death.

Like the child, the murderer lives completely inside his emotions. He has little or no ego defense against impulsively acting out the murderous fantasy. As the repressed emotions increase in violence, they explode.

On December 10, 1945, a murderer named William Heirens wrote, "For Heaven's sake catch me before I kill more. I cannot control myself."[3] His cry for help confirmed his fear of the threatening murderous explosion he might again experience.

My analysis of murderers has illuminated to a greater or lesser degree one common characteristic present in all the subjects. Each of them was tormented, yet continued to maintain a serene facade. This is why neighbors so often say of a murderer, "He was such a nice boy!" Inside that niceness or placidity, however, each one felt trapped in an intense private struggle between his drives for sexual satisfaction, independence and self-preservation and the limitations of his external surroundings.

In order to gain a better understanding of the psychology of Jack the Ripper, it would be useful to compare him with other mass murderers. Unfortunately, extensive literature in the field is lacking. No psychological scrutiny, for example, has yet been given to Charles Starkweather's series of murders committed during his wild car ride across the Plains states in 1958, or to the activities of France's infamous Dr. Marcel Petiot, who murdered and then cremated or dissected some sixty victims, mostly Jews, in 1949.

In 1977, however, I had the rare opportunity to make a lengthy first-hand examination of a mass murderer.[4] That year a series of bizarre murders shocked the inhabitants of New York along with the rest of America. Over the span of a single year, the killer murdered five young women, maimed two others, and accidentally killed one man. The killer deliberately selected as his victims young women sitting in parked cars with their dates and shot them through the head with a handgun.

For nearly a year, the New York City Police Department was unsuccessful in its attempt to locate the murderer, who had identified himself in letters to the newspapers as "Son of Sam." At last, on August 10, 1977, David Berkowitz, a mail sorter in the Bronx Post Office, was arrested for the Son of Sam murders. He killed, he said, at the behest of "voices," one of which was that of a six-thousand-year-old man named Sam, whose name he took on. He claimed he was not able to resist the demands of these inner demons.

Five days after Berkowitz's arrest, I was engaged by the prosecution to determine whether he was mentally fit to stand trial for his homicides. Two other psychiatrists had already interviewed him and pronounced him to be insane and consequently unfit to stand trial; a third would later agree with their findings.

Through extensive interviews and correspondence, I studied Berkowitz's personality, his behavior, his childhood and youth, and, later on, his home and family life. It was the first time a mass murderer, with his full cooperation, had been psychoanalyzed by a psychiatrist. I concluded that he had not been insane at the time of the murders and was therefore competent to stand trial. My conclusion was based on the fact that Berkowitz knew what he was doing when he murdered, i.e., he understood the consequences of his actions. He knew that his actions were wrong, that he might be caught and that he might go to prison. He never really heard the voices; he just said so in order to sound crazy.

There are many significant similarities between Jack the Ripper and David Berkowitz. They both achieved a kind of mythological stature from their crimes. Both murderers were under a compulsion to continue murdering. The intended victims for both were women. Berkowitz's obsession was his conviction that his victims were sexually promiscuous because they engaged in amorous embraces in the back seat of a car. (The act of killing, in fact, sexually aroused him, although he minimized this fact.) Similarly, Jack the Ripper attacked the most obviously promiscuous women in society—the street prostitutes.

Both Jack the Ripper and Son of Sam struck without warning.[5] Neither man, it appeared, had any interest in his victims as individuals; it was merely a selection of scapegoats who represented a type of sexual behavior that aroused the attacker to fury.

David Berkowitz told me he stalked his victims before he shot them, sometimes following them for hours. At times he would drive all night looking for his appropriate victim. Sometimes he gave up because the chances of being discovered were too great. It is likely that Jack the Ripper followed a similar procedure.

Although there are many parallels between Jack the Ripper and Son of Sam, closer scrutiny reveals noticeable differences in the style of the two murderers.

Jack the Ripper showed more than a casual interest in his victims. His extensive mutilation of each body required considerable lingering with his fallen prey. Son of Sam, on the other hand, depended on one shot to annihilate his victims, and then he quickly disappeared.

Ironically, Berkowitz never correlated the sound of a gunshot with the possibility of being caught. This was his undoing. Shortly after a woman heard a shot during his last attack in Brooklyn, in July 1977, she saw a man running to his car. She described the vehicle to the police, who began a thorough check of the neighborhood. The car was traced to Berkowitz. When he was arrested, fourteen days later, he had a .44 caliber gun in a paper bag, ready for another escapade.

What were David Berkowitz's feelings when he killed the women? Did he feel powerful? Did he condone his behavior? He not only approved of his actions, but was eager to elaborate on them. He reported to me, "The desire to do it, to kill, had filled me up to such explosive proportions, it caused me such turmoil inside, that when it released itself, it was like a volcano erupting, and the pressure was over—for a while anyhow."[6]

Berkowitz told me he felt exhilarated after each shooting. After his first killing, he went back to his car and sang, fully gratified—sexually, too—by the murder. I believe this sense of gratification is probably what the Ripper felt after strangling his victims and wielding the knife. The pressure cooker of anger and frustration was relieved—for a little while, at least.

While Jack the Ripper performed a long, drawn-out mutilation of his victims, Son of Sam took a hands-off approach. The Ripper carried out a ritual of postmortem desecration of his victims, which became noticeably more destructive with each ensuing murder. In sharp contrast, Berkowitz took careful aim at the women's heads with the intention of killing them immediately. Interestingly, Berkowitz did use a knife in his first attack on a woman. It proved, fortunately for the victim, to be an unsuccessful and gruesomely awkward method. Here is the account he gave me of the incident, reprinted from my book, *Confessions of Son of Sam*:

On Christmas Eve 1975, on Baychester Avenue in Co-op City in the Bronx, a 14-year-old girl was attacked and stabbed repeatedly in the back and side of the chest by an unknown assailant. Her screams attracted attention, and she was rushed to Jacobi Hospital. Her wounds, proving to be superficial, were treated and she was released. For a long time afterward, she was beset by terror, nervousness and nightmares.

I was taken quite by surprise when, at an early interview with Berkowitz, he openly confessed to me that he had committed the crime. This was news to me; he hadn't mentioned it before.

He told me: "I attacked a girl, I put a knife in her several times . . . I realized I'd stabbed her. After the stabbing I ran to my car."

"When you ran away you must have realized you did something wrong."

"Yes," he answered.

"How did you feel when you stabbed her?"

"Very strange, confused. I didn't understand what was happening to me. I tried to kill.

"That was a mess," he added. "It was a young girl. I had a small hunting knife with a blade 3½″ long. I used to go to the woods and go camping. It was late at night, about 10:30 or 11:00. I saw her immediately. In my first attempt to kill I didn't know how to do it. I stabbed her, she looked at me. I stabbed her again. It was terrible, she screamed pitifully. It wasn't like the movies when the stabbed person falls down and is killed. I kept stabbing her with the knife. She was trying to grab me. She screamed and I was getting sick. It made me sick. After a little while I just couldn't tell whether she was stabbed or I was ripping her coat. I wasn't going to rape her or take her money. I was only going to kill her. That's all."

"Isn't that enough?" I asked.

He looked down, not wanting to meet my eyes. Scared of what I might see in them, he turned his head away without a word.

The room, of a sudden, felt smaller.

How did Berkowitz appear with his camping knife, which he had described as a hunting knife? This time he was not camping, he was hunting—for a victim. Terrifying the girl, he himself was just as terrified. The scene was grotesque; there was terror in the knife. It made him sick.[7]

Although he wasn't able to murder with a knife, this first attempt was the precipitating event in the pathology of his life. Once David Berkowitz had found his true weapon—the revolver—he was able to murder easily.

Both Berkowitz and Jack the Ripper wrote messages, notes and letters to the police and media, fully intending that the publication would greatly highlight their perverted activities. Berkowitz wrote to Jimmy Breslin of the New York *Daily News*:

Hello from the gutters of N.Y.C. which are filled with dog manure, vomit, stale wine, urine and blood. Hello from the sewers of N.Y.C. . . . J.B. I am just dropping a line to let you know that I appreciate your interest in those recent and horrendous .44 killings. I also want to tell you that I read your column daily and find it quite informative.

. . . I love my work. Now the void has been filled. Not knowing what the future holds I shall say farewell and I will see you at the next job . . .

In their blood and from the gutter.

"Sam's Creation"

P.S. J.B., Please inform all the detectives working on the slayings to remain.[8]

The "Son of Sam" letters have themes in common with the Ripper correspondence. Each of the writings portrayed similar instincts and feelings, even statements such as, "I love my work," among others. Yet Berkowitz was unaware of the barrage of mail Jack the Ripper had fired at the police almost a century earlier. Examples of the Ripper letters are provided for comparison.

25 Sept., 1888 (to Central News Agency; received Thursday, September 27)

Dear Boss,

I keep on hearing the police have caught me, but they won't fix me just yet. I have laughed when they look so clever and talk about being on the right track. The joke about Leather Apron gave me real fits.

I am down on whores and I shan't quit ripping them till I do get buckled. Grand work, the last job was. I gave the lady no time to squeal. How can they catch me now? I love my work and want to start again. You will soon hear of me and my funny little games.

I saved some of the proper red stuff in a ginger beer bottle over the last job, to write with, but it went thick like glue and I can't use it. Red ink is fit enough I hope. *Ha! Ha!*

The next job I do I shall clip the lady's ears off and send them to the police, just for jolly, wouldn't you? Keep this letter back until I do a bit more work, then give it out straight. My knife's so nice and sharp, I want to get to work right away if I get a chance. Good luck,

> Yours truly,
> Jack the Ripper.

Don't mind me giving the trade name. Wasn't good enough to post this before I got all the red ink off my hands; curse it. No luck yet. They say I am a doctor now. *Ha! Ha!*

(Postcard to Central News Agency mailed October 1)

I was not codding, dear old Boss, when I gave you the tip. You'll hear about Saucy Jack's work tomorrow. Double event this time. Number one squealed a bit. Couldn't finish straight off. Had no time to get ears for police. Thanks for keeping last letter back till I go to work again.

> Jack the Ripper

(To the head of the Vigilance Committee; received October 16)

From hell
Mr. Lusk,
Sir,

    I send you half the kidne I took from one woman, prasarved it for you, tother piece I fried and ate it was very nise. I may send you the bloody knif that took it out if you only wate a whil longer.

                Signed
                Catch me when you can, Mishter Lusk.

(To Mr. Lusk)

Say Boss, you seem rare firghtened. Guess I like to give you fits, but can't stop long enough to let you box of toys play copper games with me, but hope to see you when I don't hurry too much.

                              Goodbye, Boss.

(To Mr. Lusk; received October 12, 1888)

The Boss
Central News Office
London City

I write you a letter in black ink, as I have no more of the right stuff. I think you are all asleep in Scotland Yard with your bloodhounds, as I will show you tomorrow night. I am going to do a double event but not in Whitechapel. Got rather too warm there. Had to shift. No more till you hear me again.

                              Jack the Ripper

(Envelope postmarked October 29 addressed to)

Dr. Openshaw
Pathological curator
London Hospital
Whitechapel

Old boss, you was rite it was the left kidny; i was goin to hopperate again close to your ospittle just as i was goin to dror mi nife along of er bloomin throte them cusses of coppers spoilt the game but i guess i will be on the job soon and will send you another bit of innerds

Jack the ripper

O have you seen the devle
with his mikerscope and scalpul
a lookin at a kidney
with a slide cocked up

November 9, 1888

Dear Boss
You see I have done another good thing for Whitchaple

Yours in luck
Jack the Ripper
J. F. W.

Both the Ripper and Berkowitz sent their letters by regular mail to the police or newspapers. The notes were bombastic and strongly exhibitionist. Many were obviously designed to stimulate the panic they did indeed generate. Berkowitz yearned desperately to proclaim his presence to the world; the power that lay in being able to terrify untold thousands of people was intoxicating.

Jack the Ripper was even more of an exhibitionist; he bombarded the police with messages, spelling words colloquially and phonetically and deliberately disguising his handwriting in different ways. Presumably, his intention was to give the impression that the writer was an uneducated person.

The behavior of Jack the Ripper and Son of Sam exhibits all the signs of sexual perversion. Any inquiry into the Whitechapel murders would obviously focus on a person who would have had serious emotional and sexual disturbances. I found such sexual deviation in Son of Sam; yet, the perversion reached a much higher degree in Jack the Ripper.

Just what is sexual perversion? To begin with, it is an erotic expression of hate. A perverted person is one who is consumed by a painful sexual dichotomy of desire and self-image. It is frequently the result of a poor sexual identity. In the case of Jack the Ripper and Son of Sam, both men experienced a sense of passivity or even castration in their relationships (or lack of them) with their mothers.

The absence of early nurturing experiences hindered their development of a sound masculine identity, producing a gender disorder grounded in hate and revenge. A killer steeped in such sexual disorder will not only kill, but also act out his vengeance on a woman victim.

There is a direct correlation between sexual perversion and a child's interaction with his mother. A cool, unbending and demanding mother may instill continuous fear and anxiety, which, if continued throughout formative development, will result in feelings of being passive and repressed, in other words, castrated. In fact, perversions are viewed as psychological expressions of castration.

To survive the perceived threat of his mother, the child "cuts off" his feelings; he dehumanizes his own identity as a protective shield for his sense of vulnerability and powerlessness. Women, all women, will then be viewed as repressive or overbearing, particularly in a sexual context. As sexual fantasies arise or are triggered in the presence of a woman, so does the drive to annihilate or dehumanize the source of feeling inadequate—the woman.

Do not be lulled into believing that perversion is manifested only by malcontents and murderers. As a matter of fact, we are all, in some ways, perverse. The difference is to what degree. Deviations from normal behavior, such as sodomy, bestiality, pederasty and pedophilia, are some of the activities of a perverted person. His sexual inventiveness is a consequence of the need to overcome his sense of castration and passivity. There is a persistent urge to take inordinate risks in order to challenge his wimpish self-image.

Although Jack the Ripper and Son of Sam defiantly declared

their intentions of continuing their attacks, they frequently cried out to be stopped. Their vigorous correspondence with the police and press exhibited, simultaneously, a hunger for attention and an unconscious desire to give up.

Studies of criminal behavior reveal a strong ambivalence in the minds of perpetrators. Their heinous acts against humanity produce wide swings in emotions. While engaged in the wrongdoing, the felon soars high in spirit, relishing the evil task. In retrospect, however, when he reviews the outcome of his acts, he swings down to a low point, feeling remorse and seeking penitence.

The murderer is driven to kill, partly because he craves public notice, and partly because he has secret sexual needs. Again, psychological studies of murderers indicate that a large majority are plagued by sexual conflict, specifically in the realm of their masculinity.

We may safely conclude that Jack the Ripper despised women and revenged himself in their total destruction. The extent of his feelings of inadequacy was manifested in the violent disfigurement and disembowelment of their bodies.

Jack the Ripper continued his cathartic series of assaults, ending with the murder of Marie Jeanette Kelly on November 9, 1888, and he was never caught. Nearly a century later, on August 10, 1977, Berkowitz was arrested before he could kill again.

1. David Abrahamsen, M.D., *The Murdering Mind*, Harper & Row, New York, 1973, p. 1.
2. *Ibid.*, p. 10.
3. Michael Newton, *Hunting Humans. An Encyclopedia of Modern Serial Killers*, Loompanic Unlimited, Port Townsend, WA, p. 154.
4. David Abrahamsen, M.D., *Confessions of Son of Sam*, Columbia University Press, New York, 1985, p. 2.
5. *Ibid.*, p. 88.
6. *Ibid.*, p. 70.
7. *Ibid.*, pp. 89–90.
8. New York *Daily News*, June 5, 1977, p. 8.

CHAPTER THREE

A Well-Balanced Ignorance of Jack the Ripper and Freud

"Lord, what fools these mortals be!"

SHAKESPEARE,
A *Midsummer Night's Dream*,
III, ii

ONE OF THE most extraordinary legacies of the Jack the Ripper murders is literary. For the past one hundred years, there has been an outpouring of books and plays about the Ripper story, which have created a kind of mythology on top of the mystery.

To some extent, the mass of nebulous writings may have contributed to the mystique that surrounds Jack the Ripper. Most of the literature is in the nature of what might be called descriptive thrillers, which have never sought to explicate the psychodynamics of this cruel drama. The one-dimensional, static descriptions have attempted to exploit the story's most bizarre elements without furnishing any insight into the reason—or unreason—behind the murders.

But years of research work in psychoanalysis and the abnormal aspects of criminal behavior have taught me one important lesson. No case is so bizarre or mysterious that it cannot, within certain

limits, be unraveled. In fact, I have found that the more excep-
tional, the more unnatural the case may appear, the less mysterious it will turn out to be when subjected to careful examination.

To take one example, my deliberate scrutiny of Son of Sam's life
and his emotional background eventually revealed the secrets of
his mind and behavior. Every murderer is just like the rest of us in
that he has individual psychosocial characteristics that are
founded upon the structure of his family, his experiences with the
family, and his emotional reactions to that immediate environment. For each person, those characteristics are unique.

Unfortunately, at the time of the Whitechapel murders, concepts of the mind and how it functions were virtually nonexistent
to help understand the murderous behavior of Jack the Ripper.
Only recently has our scrutiny of people's conduct been enlight-
ened by an understanding of their emotional development.

We like to believe that our inner life is orderly and that our
behavior and actions are always logical. But even our most trivial
activities are associated with our unconscious feelings. Our mixing
up or forgetting dates and names, our misplacing objects, our
everyday slips of the tongue or pen, all indicate how our unconscious interferes with our conscious emotions. This is the essence
of Sigmund Freud's theory. [1]

When he made the epoch-making discovery of the mind's
unconscious power, Sigmund Freud laid the groundwork for understanding human behavior in general and criminal conduct in
particular. Although he did not devote his time specifically to the
study of the criminal mind, he revealed, as early as 1906, in a
lecture entitled "Psycho-Analysis and the Ascertaining of Truths
in the Courts of Law," that "in the case of a criminal it [truth or
reason] is a secret which he knows and hides from you, but in the
case of a neurotic it is a secret hidden from him." [2] Later, he
rephrased this: "With the neurotic the secret is hidden from his
own consciousness; with the criminal it is hidden only from you." [3]

Freud emphasized that the unconscious was the force behind all human behavior—investigating, controlling or releasing every action. In the unconscious lie our wishes, fears, dreams and longings. Alongside are our accumulated frustrations and broken hopes, which sometimes overshadow our constructive actions and take control of our behavior.

Although Freud's theories sounded strange at the time, present day clinical practice has, to a large extent, confirmed their validity. Clarifying the emotional relationship between child and parent, particularly in relation to oedipal circumstances, is the underlying theme in emotional development as well as the foundation for the theory of psychoanalysis.

Social behavior is modified through sublimation, a process by which infantile sexual expressions and aggressive pleasures are repressed in order to meet the requirements of adulthood. Maturity, as we deem it to be, is a finely-tuned combination of independence and control of hostile and destructive tendencies. Psychoanalysis, to the extent possible, is a science of the relationship between the mind and the body.

Because criminal behavior always involves secret elements, the role of the unconscious emotions is pivotal in discovering from where and when such hidden motivation evolves.

Unraveling the secrets of the Ripper was a task I found especially challenging. For one thing, all the actual facts about the case had been entombed in various English and American archives. For another, the murderer's identity had never been established. And, even if it were known, there was no possibility of being able to summon him back from the grave for personal psychoanalytic interviews.

I continued to compile information as and when I could. Months became years. The mass of materials grew. I spent months delving into the Victorian underworld and the fascination it exerted on the more fortunate members of that society, so riven by class distinctions.

I kept coming back to the same questions. Where did Jack the

Ripper come from? Who were his parents? Was he married? Where did he live? And how did he earn his livelihood? At each turn, I faced another wall in the maze of contradictory material and narrative hyperbole. Like the public of the Ripper's day, I was tantalized by the total lack of factual information about the man himself.

First I had to find out how the murders were committed, what was actually done to the bodies, who the women were. Then I had to sort through the many cards and letters signed "Jack the Ripper." Some, it seems, were the work of publicity-hungry amateurs, who hoped to capture a piece of the abundant news limelight arising from public preoccupation with the murders. A few hand-writing experts declared that some of the correspondence was written by the same man, even though the Ripper disguised his handwriting and spelled words differently in each one.

At the time of the Whitechapel murders there were no crimi-nological laboratories as we know them today. Postmortem an-alyses, although conducted with scrupulous care and recorded in detail, were, nevertheless, insufficient, due to a cursory use of the microscope. Scientific scrutiny of blood, hair and handwriting was outside the scope of Victorian technological methods. Anal-ysis of fingerprints or fibers from clothing was unperfected and limited.

Despite the absence of sophisticated investigative techniques, forensic medicine and pathology were thriving specialties. Scien-tific examinations of the components of a crime gained esteem from highly reputable institutes in Edinburgh, Glasgow and Lon-don. However, forensic application was of little value without serological or microscopic determinations of blood, hair or semen. Had blood groupings been possible at the time of the Ripper murders, an analysis might well have provided valuable clues. A finding of semen in the mouth or in the rectum of the victim could have indicated the nature of the murderer's sexual behavior.[4]

Although science helps us understand human behavior, it is not

47

sufficient. In order to solve the Ripper mystery, we have to explore, besides the historical facts, the circumstantial evidence and emotional linkages in the Whitechapel murders. Science constitutes a cornerstone for understanding human conduct, but is not sufficient to pinpoint the whole truth. We need to search out the obscure facts and then grasp their meaning. It is useful to hail science; yet it is wise to remember the caveat of Ludwig Wittgenstein that the usefulness of the scientific method is limited.[5]

The obscure facts in the Whitechapel murders were not easily accessible and their importance could be easily overlooked. Below the surface or conscious level of one's perception is another kind of truth or knowledge that we do not understand. We sometimes label that knowledge as instinct or "gut feelings." I call it the poetic truth.

Whatever is learned of a person's behavior leading to murderous activities is based upon our fundamental medical and psychiatric-psychological theories, which, in turn, depend upon years of observation, training and experience. I began by extracting certain names from the litany of suspects. Then I applied the psychobiological elements of behavior, accompanied by the psychohistorical hints along the murky road to the murders.

In 1843, England became the first country to modify its criminal law to allow an insanity defense. The so-called "McNaghten Rule" came from a seminal case involving a man named Daniel McNaghten who suffered from the delusion that Sir Robert Peel wanted to kill him. In attempting the assassination of Peel, McNaghten shot and killed Peel's secretary. He was charged with murder but acquitted by the jury on the grounds of insanity. A new principle had been laid down in this case that would have a great bearing on British and American jurisprudence. Insanity was defined as a state of mind in which the accused did not know the nature and quality of his act or, if he did, that he did not know that what he was doing was wrong.[6]

As an example of the underworkings of a disturbed mind, we

will turn to the circumstances surrounding the Ripper's third victim. Elizabeth Stride had not been mutilated. One reason may have been that he was warned that somebody was coming and was required, unwillingly, to abandon his usual carving up of his victim. The tone of the postcard sent on October 1, 1888, to Central News Agency reflected a kind of cockiness—as if the interruption of the carnal desecration was really to his liking. He conveyed his arrogance by trying to give the impression he had completed what he had set out to do. That, of course, was not the case.

The interruption created an urgency to kill again, to complete the pattern of his murderous attacks. Later that same night, he murdered Catherine Eddowes, this time with all the grandiose touches of his sadistic aggression. He took no time for any further selection of locale. Eddowes's mutilated body also was found within the City limits, no more than half a mile from where the Ripper had left Stride's body. Now, the murders involved the City of London Police as well as the Metropolitan force.

In 1888, with emotions at an almost unbearable pitch, the populace demanded that the perpetrator of the brutal murders be found and eradicated. The public cared little about understanding the criminal's behavior or the aberrant characteristics driving him toward his prey. Throughout all the detective work carried out to identify Jack the Ripper and to figure out his behavior, there was one glaring lack in the approach, the question: How did his mind work? But, to comprehend such a mind—the criminal mind—was beyond the ken of the investigators.

The Ripper did not anticipate being surprised during the murder of Elizabeth Stride. In a postcard to the police he noted, "Thanks for keeping last letter back till I go to work again."

He was referring to a card sent four days earlier and prior to Stride's murder. The police had chosen not to publish the card, in contrast to what they had done with the other communications. It was a new tactic in coping with this anonymous and elusive murderer. They may have hoped that when his card was not acknowledged, the murderer would become anxious and angry and, driven by his need for attention and recognition, give himself up. The plan did not work.

The fact that the writer communicated intensively and eagerly with public authorities demonstrated, however, his ambiguity in considering the murders his private domain, his possession, a part of his existence. To this self-confident, arrogant personality, the ability to have killed without being discovered, to have eluded every attempt to catch him and to have outwitted the entire London police force meant nothing unless everyone knew about it. These deeds, which would never be forgotten, had become his calling card for immortality.

Mingled with this craving for attention was an unconscious wish to be stopped. By announcing who he was in these communications, he challenged the police to uncover his identity. Such bloody work, which originated while he was in an excited, manic stage, would culminate in guilt and depression. These severe fluctuations in emotional behavior are common psychological symptoms among murderers.

Early in the nineteenth century, Immanuel Kant stated, "Before the earth perishes, the last thief should be hanged with the guts of the last murderer."[7] You may be surprised to learn that Kant was considered one of the more liberal-minded philosophers. Such a harsh and uncomprehending attitude toward the criminal was prevalent in Britain, as well as in other countries that regarded themselves as civilized. That view, of course, was completely antithetical to any meaningful investigation of the underlying causes for murder.

The Ripper was depicted as a madman who acted alone. The newspaper accounts of his swift homicides and even faster disappearances were considered signs of a sole and self-directed murderer. His almost magical power to appear and then suddenly disappear was terrifying.

Murder is usually a solitary act—but not always. I had analyzed a collaborative homicide in the case of Nathan Leopold and Richard Loeb, who, in 1924, when they were both eighteen years old, had killed a fourteen-year-old boy, Bobby Frank. They were sentenced to life plus ninety-nine years imprisonment for kidnapping and murder.

I saw Leopold first in 1941 when I worked at the Diagnostic Depot in the Illinois State Penitentiary in Joliet, and later on when I came to play a direct role in what was left of his life. The crux of the so-called perfect murder the two of them planned, and the feature that made the vicious crime understandable, was the intense homosexual relationship between Leopold and Loeb. Underlying the murder was a strong sexual current, where one urged the other to kill. Likely, too, there was abuse of the young victim's body, a factor that went unrecognized.[8]

What motivates a murderer is a combination of frustrations, fears and depression, deeply rooted in his past. Such a broad concept, however, is not sufficient to explain how the urge to kill dominates a murderer's mind. My years of psychiatric practice have taught me that human behavior frequently fails to conform to our inadequate theories because the intimate connection the murderer feels to his victim may not have been fully explored.

A very important factor is the murderer's emotional relationship with other men, which may fuel his hatred, especially toward women. In a homosexual relationship, strong ties develop that intensify hostile and destructive feelings to such an extent that they become murderous. Frequently, one partner may incite the other into daring acts, which the other is willing to do to please or keep the attention of his lover.

In 1913, Charles Goring asserted that certain criminal tendencies are discernible among the general behavior patterns of human beings.[9] It would be a long time, however, before this view would be incorporated into understanding the human interactions of feeling, motivation and behavior.

1. David Abrahamsen, M.D., *The Road to Emotional Maturity*, Prentice Hall, New York, 1958.
2. Lecture delivered to Prof. Loffler's Seminar in June, 1906. First published in the *Archiv fur Kriminalanthropologie und Kriminalstatistik*, von H. Gross, 1906.
3. Reprinted in *Collected Papers*, Vol. 11, by Sigmund Freud, M.D., LL.D., The Hogarth Press, London, and the Institute of Psycho-Analysis, 1942, pp. 18, 21.
4. William C. Eckert, M.D. "The Whitechapel Murders. The Case of Jack the Ripper," *The American Journal of Forensic Medicine and Pathology*. Vol. 2, No. 1, March, 1981, pp. 58, 59.
5. Ray Monk, *The Duty of Genius*, Free Press, New York, 1990, p. 63.
6. David Abrahamsen, M.D., *Crime and the Human Mind*, Columbia University Press, New York, 1944, p. 4.
7. *Ibid.*, p. 73.
8. David Abrahamsen, M.D., *Ibid.*, p. 163, and *The Mind of the Accused. A Psychiatrist in the Courtroom*, Simon & Schuster, New York, 1983, p. 48.
9. Charles Goring, *The English Convict*, Prison Commission, Home Office, London, 1913, p. 173.

PART TWO

WHAT THE INQUESTS REVEALED

CHAPTER FOUR

Murder Cases Unfolding

"I plucked a violet from my mother's grave, when a boy . . ."

Song Marie Jeanette Kelly was
singing the night she was
killed, as revealed at the
inquest.

B Y THE TIME 1888 had ended—described by Queen Victoria as "this new strange year of three eights that could never be written again"[1]—the inquests on the Whitechapel murders had brought forth a mass of detailed information about the killings and the victims. The way the murder situations played out, one after the other, emerges from the materials contained in the Scotland Yard files. On the surface, each would seem to have been initially a sexual encounter that abruptly turned into appalling violence. The price had shifted from the half crown or even four shillings that was a prostitute's fee in those days, to death and mutilation.

The first problem facing the coroner and jury at the inquests was identifying the victims. This was not easy, since the women moved constantly from one lodging house to another and were without a regular job. Though the police tried hard to locate the women's relatives, they found it almost impossible because the victims were often estranged from their families, or the relatives were ashamed to come forward and report the victims as missing. Meanwhile, the public was hammering at the police to catch the murderer, who had left no identifying evidence.

Faced with this Herculean task, the police could not entirely be blamed for their unsuccessful search for the murderer. Detailing the case of Marie Jeanette Kelly may illuminate the complications faced by Scotland Yard and its inadequate police force. At the same time, Kelly's story illustrates the tragedy of circumstances that led to the downfall of all the Ripper's victims.

She was only twenty-five years old. Had the cards been dealt differently, she may have achieved a way to better herself. She was the last and youngest of the Ripper's victims, and the only one of the five who was murdered in her own room. Details of her life and behavior revealed after her death indicated a sense of self-respect and caring. If a caste structure existed among prostitutes, she may have been slotted in a higher status than her more degraded associates.

The inquest on Marie Jeanette Kelly began on November 12, 1888. An article in the *Daily Telegraph* on November 10, 1888, the day after her death, provided a view of Dorset Street and the adjoining Paternoster Row, Kelly's surroundings. The streets, which led directly to the Spitalfields vegetable market,

have now been given up to common lodging houses at 4d. and 6d. a night . . . and to women who have lost every trace of womanliness. The street and the row are places which the police state are hardly safe for any respectable person by day and certainly not at night. In such a neighbourhood it was impossible to rise; to sink lower was inevitable. Evidence tends to show that when Kelly first made its acquaintance respectable friends still looked after and wrote to her. It is the uniform testimony of local authorities that these evil surroundings are only remedied by wholesale demolitions, and that while they exist moral agencies are almost hopeless. They are whirlpools, and the poor and the wretched are dragged into them. Though the police report that Kelly's father lives in Wales, there seems no doubt that she is Irish, and McCarthy [Kelly's landlord] states that the letters for her used to come from some part of Ireland.[2]

We learn more about Marie Kelly's life when we get to know Joseph Barnett, the man with whom she had recently been living. Because he was initially late in reporting his knowledge of her to the police, they had begun to suspect him of involvement in Kelly's murder. He was the first witness called to testify on November 12, and having been sworn, deposed as follows:

(As the inquest transcript is unpunctuated, I have added some punctuation to clarify it.)

I reside at 24 and 25 New Street Bishopsgate which is a common lodging house. I am a laborer & have been a fish porter. I now live at my sisters, 21 Portpool Lane, Grays Inn Road. I have lived with the deceased one year and eight months. Her name was Marie Jeanette Kelly. Kelly was her maiden name and the name she always went by. I have seen the body. I identify her by the ear and the eyes. I am positive it is the same woman. I have lived with her at 13 room Millers Court eight months or longer. I separated from her on the 30th of October. I left her because she had a person who was a prostitute whom she took in and I objected to her doing so, that was the only reason, not because I was out of work. I left her on the 30th October between 5 & 6 P.M. I last saw her alive between 7.30 & 7.45 the night of Thursday before she was found. I was with her about one hour, we were on friendly terms. I told her when I left her I had no work and had nothing to give her of which I was very sorry. We did not drink together, she was quite sober, she was as long as she was with me of sober habits, she has got drunk several times in my presence . . .

She had one sister . . . and six brothers at home and one was in the army . . . She told me she had been married when very young in Wales, she was married to a collier she told me the name was Davis or Davies. She told me she was lawfully married to him until he died in an explosion. She said she lived with him 2 or 3 years up to his death. She told me she was married at the age of 16 years. She came to London about 4 years ago, after her husband's death. She said she first went to Cardiff and was in an infirmary there 8 or 9 months and followed a bad life with a cousin whilst in Cardiff. When she left Cardiff she said she came to London. In London she was first in a gay house in the West End of the Town. A gentleman there asked her to go to France . . . [but] she did not like it and returned. She came back and lived in Ratcliffe Highway for some time, she did not tell me how long. Then she was living near Stepney Gas Works. Morganstone was the man she lived with there, she did not tell me how long she lived there . . . and later with another man, Joseph Fleming, she was very fond of him . . .

I picked up with her in Commercial Street Spitalfields. The first night we had a drink together and I arranged to see her the next day and then Saturday we agreed to remain together and I took lodging in George Street where I was known. I lived there with her till I left her the other day. She had on several occasions asked me to read about the murders. She seemed to be afraid of someone, she did not express fear of any particular individual except when she roomed with me but away we came to terms quickly. [3]

The *Daily Telegraph* reported on November 13, 1888, that the coroner appreciated and believed the evidence given by Barnett. At that point, it became apparent that Barnett was no longer suspected of having killed Marie. [4]

There was considerable disagreement among the witnesses about whether any screams for help had been heard from Kelly's room. The inquest records one witness, Elizabeth Prater, who, having been sworn, gave evidence as follows:

I am the wife of William Prater a Boot Machinist he has deserted me for 5 years. I live at No. 20 Room Millers Court up stairs. I lived in the room over where deceased lived.

On Thursday I went into the Court about 5 o'clock in the evening and returned about 1 on Friday Morning. I stood at the corner by Mr. McCarthys shop till about 20 minutes past 1. I spoke

The Jack the Ripper
public house was
likely frequented by
the Ripper's victims
and the Ripper
himself when it was
known as The Ten
Bells.

to no one I was waiting for a man I lived with, he did not come. I
went up to my room. On the stairs I could see a glimmer through
the partition if there had been a light in the deceaseds room I might
not have noticed it. I did not take particular notice. I could have
heard her moving if she had moved.

I went in about 1.30. I put 2 tables against the door. I went to
sleep at once. I had had something to drink. I slept soundly till a
Kitten disturbed me about 3.30 to 4. I noticed the lodging light was
out, so it was after 4 probably. I heard a cry of oh! Murder! as the cat
came on me and I pushed her down, the voice was in a faint voice.
The noise seemed to come from close by. It is nothing uncommon
to hear cries of Murder so I took no notice. I did not hear it a second
time. I heard nothing else whatever. I went to sleep again and woke
at 5 o'clock.

I got up and went down and went across to the ten bells [the local beer-shop, the Ten Bells] I was there at ¼ to 6 at the corner of Church Street. I saw several men harnessing horses in Dorset Street. Mary Ann Cox [another witness] could have passed down the Court during the night without me hearing her. After having a drink at the 10 Bells I went home and slept till 11.

I went to bed at half past one—I did not hear any singing. I should have heard anyone singing in deceased's room at 1 o'clock; there was no one singing.[5]

During Mrs. Prater's testimony, according to the *Daily Telegraph* of November 12, 1888, the coroner asked her, "Do you often hear cries of murder?" and she replied, "It is nothing unusual in the street. I did not take particular notice."

Did you hear it a second time?—No.

Did you hear beds or tables being pulled about?—None whatever. I went asleep, and was awake again at five A.M. I passed down the stairs, and saw some men harnessing horses. At a quarter to six I was in the Ten Bells.

Could the witness, Mary Ann Cox, have come down the entry between one and half-past one o'clock without your knowledge?—Yes, she could have done so.

Did you see any strangers at the Ten Bells?—No, I went back to bed and slept until eleven.

You heard no singing downstairs?—None whatever. I should have heard the singing distinctly. It was quite quiet at half-past one o'clock.[6]

Another witness, Sarah Lewis, testified as follows:

I live at 24 Great Powell Street Spitalfields. I am a laundress. I knew Mrs. Keyler in Millers Court. I was at her house at half past 2 on Friday Morning. She lives at No 2 in the Court on the left on the first floor. I know the time by having looked at Spitalfields Church Clock as I passed it. When I went in the Court I saw a man opposite the Court in Dorset Street standing alone by the Lodging House. He was not tall—but stout—had on a wideawake black hat—I did not notice his clothes. Another young man with a woman passed along. The man standing in the street was looking up the court as if waiting for some one to come out, I went to Mrs. Keylers. I was awake all night in a chair. I dozed. I heard no noise. I woke up at about half past three. I heard the clock strike half past three. I sat awake till nearly five. A little before 4 I heard a female voice shout loudly once Murder! The sound seemed to come from the direction of deceaseds room. There was only one scream. I took no notice of it. I left Mrs. Keylers at about half past 5 in the afternoon. The police would not let us out before.

About Wednesday night at 8 o'clock I was going along Bethnal Green Road with another female and a Gentleman passed us he turned back & spoke to us. He asked us to follow him, and asked one of us he did not mind which. We refused, he went away, and came back & said if we would follow him he would treat us. He asked us to go down a passage. He had a bag, he put it down saying What are you frightened of?; He then undid his coat and felt for something and we ran away. He was short, pale faced, with a black small moustache, about 40 years of age. The bag he had was about a foot or nine inches long. He had on a round high hat—a high one for a round—he had a brownish long overcoat and a short black coat underneath—and pepper & salt trousers.

On our running away we did not look after the man. On the Friday morning about half past two when I was coming to Millers Court I met the same man with a female—in Commercial Street near Mr. Ringers public house, near the Market. He had then no overcoat on, but he had the bag & the same hat trowsers & undercoat. I passed by them and looked back at the man. I was frightened. I looked again when I got to the corner of Dorset Street. I have not seen the man since. I should know him if I did.[7]

In her evidence, Sarah Lewis also stated that she heard a woman's voice shout "Murder!" loudly, at a little before 4:00 A.M. on that Friday, November 9.[8]

Mary Ann Cox made a lengthy statement about Marie Jeanette Kelly:

I am a widow and live at No. 5 Room Millers Court the last house top of the Court. I get my living on the streets as best I can. I have known the female occupying No. 13 room 8 or 9 months as Mary Jane. I last saw her alive about midnight on Thursday, very much intoxicated, in Dorset Street. She went up the court a few steps in front of me, there was a short stout man shabbily dressed with her. He had a longish coat, very shabby dark and a pot of ale in his hand. He had a hard billycock black hat on. He had a blotchy face and a fully carrotty mustache, his chin was clean.

I saw them go into her room, I said good night Mary and the man banged the door, he had nothing in his hands but a pot of beer. She answered me, I am going to have a song. I went into my room and I heard her sing "a violet I plucked from mothers grave when a boy." I remained a quarter of an hour in my room, then went out. She was still singing. I returned about one o'clock. She was singing then. I warmed my hands and went out again, she was still singing. I came in again at 3 o'clock, the light was out and there was no noise. I did not undress at all that night. I heard no noise, it was raining hard. I did not go to sleep at all. I heard nothing whatever after one o'clock . . . I heard men going in and out, several go in and out. I heard some one go out at a quarter to six. I do not know what house he went out of. I heard no door shut, he did not pass my window.[9]

The *Daily Telegraph* noted some important additional questions and answers by Mary Ann Cox:[10]

How many men live in the court who work in Spitalfields Market?—One. At a quarter-past six I heard a man go down the court. That was too late for the market.

From what house did he go?—I don't know.

Did you hear the door bang after him?—No.

Then he must have walked up the court and back again?—Yes.

It might have been a policeman?—It might have been.

What would you take the stout man's age to be?—Six-and-thirty.

Did you notice the colour of his trousers?—All his clothes were dark.

Did his boots sound as if the heels were heavy?—

There was no sound as he went up the court.

Then you think that his boots were down at heels?—He made no noise.

What clothes had Mary Jane on?—She had no hat; a red pelerine [a narrow cape] and a shabby skirt.

You say she was drunk?—I did not notice she was drunk until she said good night. The man closed the door.

By the Jury: There was a light in the window, but I saw nothing, as the blinds were down. I should know the man again, if I saw him.

By the Coroner: I feel certain if there had been the cry of "Murder" in the place I should have heard it; there was not the least noise. I have often seen the woman the worse for drink.

It is difficult to reconcile the accounts of these three witnesses. A loud cry of "Murder!" was heard by the witness Sarah Lewis a little before 4:00 A.M. on Friday morning, while Elizabeth Prater heard a faint cry of "Murder!" a little after 4 A.M. Mary Ann Cox said Kelly was singing for quite a while, from soon after she came home until some time around 1:00 A.M., when Cox again left the court. Since Kelly was drunk at the time, we may also assume she might have been singing quite loudly. Yet Elizabeth Prater reported hearing no sound when she returned to Miller's Court about that time. When Mary Ann Cox came back at 3:00 A.M., she found everything dark and quiet, and though she subsequently sat up all night without sleeping, she heard no noise or cry of "Murder!"

These discrepancies could be accounted for by the fact that Whitechapel was an extremely noisy area and screams of all kinds were so often heard that people paid little attention to them. As Elizabeth Prater noted, "It [cries of Murder] is nothing unusual in the street. I did not take particular notice."

I am inclined to believe that the murder took place around 4:00 A.M., but was not discovered before 11:00 A.M. that same morning. We learn how Kelly's body was found from the evidence given at the inquest by John McCarthy:

> I am a grocer and lodging house keeper at 27 Dorset Street. On Friday morning last about 1/4 to 11 I sent my man Bowyer to fetch rent from No. 13 room Millers Court. He came back in about 5 minutes and said Governor I knocked at the door and could not make any one answer. I looked through the window and saw a lot of blood. I went out with him and looked through the window and saw the body and everything. I said to my man don't tell any one let us fetch the police. I knew deceased as Mary Jane Kelly. I have seen the body and have no doubt as to the identity. I and Bowyer went then to the Police Court Commercial Street and saw Inspector Beck. I enquired first for other inspectors. I told Inspector Beck what I had seen. He put on his hat and coat and came with me at once. Deceased has lived in the room with Joe for 10 months both together. They lived comfortably together but once broke the two windows. The furniture and everything in the room belongs to me. I was paid 4/6d. a week for the room but rent was 28/- [28 shillings] in arrear. The rent was paid to me weekly, the room was let weekly.
>
> I very often saw deceased worse for drink. She was a very quiet woman when sober but noisy when in drink. She was not ever helpless when drunk. [11]

Thomas Bowyer's observations, according to the *Daily Telegraph*, included the following: [12]

> Charles Ledger, an inspector of police, G Division, produced a plan of the premises. Bowyer pointed out the window, which was the one nearest the entrance. He continued: There was a curtain. I put my

hand through the broken pane and lifted the curtain. I saw two pieces of flesh lying on the table.

Where was this table?—In front of the bed, close to it. The second time I looked I saw a body on this bed, and blood on the floor. I at once went very quietly to Mr. McCarthy. We then stood in the shop and I told him what I had seen. We both went to the police-station, but first of all we went to the window, and McCarthy looked in to satisfy himself. We told the inspector at the police-station of what we had seen. Nobody else knew of the matter. The inspector returned with us.

Did you see the deceased constantly?—I have often seen her. I knew the last witness, Barnett. I have seen the deceased drunk once.

By the Jury: When did you see her last alive?—On Wednesday afternoon, in the court, when I spoke to her. McCarthy's shop is at the corner of Miller's Court.

Another neighbor, Julia Venturney, of No. 1 Room Miller's Court, gave the following account of what she knew of Kelly and Kelly's last night alive:

I am a charwoman, I live with Harry Owen. I knew the female who occupied No. 13 room. She said she was a married woman and her name was Kelly. She lived with Joe Barnett. She frequently got drunk. Joe Barnett would not let her go on the streets. Deceased said she was fond of another man named Joe who used to come and see her and give her money. I think he was a costermonger. She said she was very fond of him.

I last saw her alive on Thursday about 10 A.M. having her breakfast with another woman in her own room. I went to bed on Thursday night about 8 o'clock. I could not sleep all night, I only dozed. I heard no noise in the court. I heard no singing. I heard no scream. Deceased often sung Irish songs. [13]

The next witness, Maria Harvey, was the friend, another prostitute, whom Marie Kelly had taken in, and who had become the

65

reason for Joe Barnett's breaking off his relationship with her at the end of October. In her testimony, she deposed:

> I live at No. 3 New Court, Dorset Street. I knew deceased as Mary Jane Kelly. I slept two nights with her on Monday & Tuesday nights last I slept with her. We were together all the afternoon on Thursday. I am a Laundress. I was in the room when Joe Barnett called. I went away. I left my bonnet there. I knew Barnett.
>
> I left some clothes in the room, 2 men's shirts, 1 Boys shirt, and overcoat a black one a man's, a black crape bonnet with black strings, a ticket for a shawl in [pawn shop] for 2/- [two shillings]. One little childs white petticoat. I have seen nothing of them since except the overcoat produced to me by the police. I was a friend of deceaseds. She never told me of being afraid of any one. [14]

The murder of Marie Kelly caused considerable panic and several experts were called in by Scotland Yard. Among these were Dr. George Bagster Phillips, M Division's police surgeon, who had performed the postmortem on Annie Chapman, Dr. Thomas Bond, the consulting surgeon to A Division, and Dr. F. G. Brown, one of the City of London police surgeons who had reported on the body of Catherine Eddowes. Dr. Phillips's evidence, according to the inquest account, was as follows:

> I am a surgeon to M Division of the Metropolitan Police and reside at 2 Spital Square. I was called by the police on Friday morning last about 11 o'clock and proceeded to Millers Court, which I entered at 11.15 A.M. I found a room the door of which led out of the passage near 26 Dorset Street and having two windows in the Court—2 of the panes in the window nearest the passage were broken and finding the door locked I looked through the lower broken pane and satisfied myself that the mutilated corpse lying on the bed was not in need of any immediate attention from me, and I also came to the conclusion that there was nobody else on the bed or within view to whom I could render any professional assistance.

Having ascertained that probably it was advisable that no entrance should be made into the room at that time, I remained until
about 1.30 when the door was broken open, I think by Mr. McCarthy, I think by direction of Superintendent Arnold, who had arrived . . .[15]

The rest of his findings centered around the corpse of Marie
Jeanette Kelly:

The mutilated remains of a female were lying two thirds over
towards the edge of the bedstead, nearest the door of entry. She had
only her under linen garment on her, and from my subsequent
examination I am sure the body had been removed subsequent to
the injury which caused her death from that side of the bedstead
which was nearest the wooden partition. The large quantity of
blood under the bedstead, the saturated condition of the pil-
lowcase, pillow, sheet, at that top corner nearest the partition leads
me to the conclusion that the severance of the right carotid artery
which was the immediate cause of her death was inflicted while the
deceased was lying at the right side of the bedstead and her head
and neck in the top right hand corner.[16]

According to the account in the *Daily Telegraph*, Dr. Phillips
deliberately refrained from giving any more information than was
necessary for the jury to determine the cause of death. "The
police, and with them the divisional surgeon," said the report,
"have arrived at the conclusion that it is the interest of justice not
to disclose the details of the professional inquiry."[17]

It appeared, however, that death had been caused by severing
the throat, and that the mutilation had been performed subsequently. There were no signs of a struggle. A large knife had been
used. Kelly's clothes, including a velvet bodice, were on a chair by
the fireplace.[18]

The discrepancies in testimony mounted. So far, no one could
establish the time when the attack on Kelly actually took place.

Although two of the women heard cries of "Murder!" at about the same time, other witnesses heard no sound at all. Various men were seen or heard entering or leaving Miller's Court, but none could be positively identified. The man who entered the room with Kelly was carrying a pot of beer. But the next morning, neither pot nor beer was found in the room. Naturally, the man could have drunk the beer and taken the jug with him. Could he have been the murderer?

The most surprising witness of all was Caroline Maxwell, whose evidence tended to obfuscate the matter further. She testified that she had seen Marie Kelly alive hours after the murder had supposedly taken place:

I live at 14 Dorset Street. My husband's name is Harry Maxwell. He is a Lodging House Deputy. I knew deceased for about 4 months as Mary Jane. I also knew Joe Barnett. I believe she was an unfortunate girl. I never spoke to her except twice.

I took a deal of notice of deceased this evening [inquest recorder's mistake for "morning"] seeing her standing at the corner of the Court on Friday from 8 to half past. I know the time by taking the plates my husband had to take care of from the house opposite. I am positive the time was between 8 & half past. I am positive I saw deceased. I spoke to her. I said Why Mary. What brings you up so early. She said Oh! I do feel so bad! Oh Carry I feel so bad! She knew my name. I asked her to have a drink, she said Oh no I have just had a drink of ale and have brought it all up. It was in the road. I saw it. As she said this she motioned with her head and I concluded she meant she had been to the Brittania at the corner. I left her saying I pitied her feelings. I then went to Bishopsgate as I returned I saw her outside the Brittania talking to a man. The time was then about 20 minutes to half an hour later, about a quarter to nine. I could not describe the man. I did not pass them. I went into my house. I saw them in the distance, I am certain it was deceased. The man was not a tall man. He had on dark clothes and a sort of plaid coat. I could not say what hat he had on. Mary Jane had a dark skirt, velvet body, and marone [maroon] shawl and no hat.

I have seen deceased in drink but not really drunk.

By a Juror—I did not notice whether deceased [again, recorder's slip for "the man"] had on a high silk hat. If it had been so I should have noticed it I think.[19]

Caroline Maxwell's testimony was as surprising to me as it must have been to the coroner and jury at the inquest. Had she really seen the supposedly dead Marie Kelly alive that Friday morning, or was she deluded into thinking so?

The *Daily Telegraph* account of the inquest (November 13, 1888) adds some interesting additional information. We learn that Maxwell, prior to testifying "that she knew the deceased for about four months and that she spoke to her on two occasions that morning," had been cautioned by the coroner that "You must be very careful about your evidence, because it is different to other people's":[20]

You say you saw her standing at the corner of the entry to the court?—Yes, on Friday morning, from eight to half past eight. I fix the time by my husband's finishing work. When I came out of the lodging-house she was opposite.

Did you speak to her?—Yes; it was an unusual thing to see her up. She was a young woman who never associated with any one. I spoke across the street, "What, Mary, brings you up so early?" She said, "Oh, Carrie, I do feel so bad."

And yet you say you had only spoken to her twice previously; you knew her name and she knew yours?—Oh, yes; by being about in the lodging-house.

What did she say?—She said, "I've had a glass of beer, and I've brought it up again" and it was in the road. I imagined she had been in the Britannia beer-shop at the corner of the street. I left her, saying that I could pity her feelings. I went to Bishopsgate Street to

69

get my husband's breakfast. Returning I saw her outside the Britannia public-house, talking to a man.

This would be about what time?—Between eight and nine o'clock. I was absent about half an hour. It was about a quarter to nine.

What description can you give of this man?—I could not give you any, as they were at some distance.

Inspector Abberline: The distance is about sixteen yards.

Witness: I am sure it was the deceased. I am willing to swear it.

The Coroner: You are sworn now. Was he a tall man?—No; he was a little taller than me and stout.

Inspector Abberline: On consideration I should say the distance was twenty-five yards.

The Coroner: What clothes had the man?—Witness: Dark clothes; he seemed to have a plaid coat on. I could not say what sort of hat he had.

What sort of dress had the deceased?—A dark skirt, a velvet body, a maroon shawl, and no hat.

Have you ever seen her the worse for drink?—I have seen her in drink, but she was not a notorious character.

By the Jury: I should have noticed if the man had had a tall silk hat, but we are accustomed to see men of all sorts with women. I should not like to pledge myself to the kind of hat.

Maxwell's evidence, which she insisted was correct, had disrupted the investigation. Marie Jeanette Kelly was as dead as could be. She had been found with her nose cut off, forehead and left leg skinned, breasts amputated, abdomen opened, her liver by her feet and intestines draped over the mirror. Poor Joe Barnett had only been able to identify the pitiful body in the mortuary by her ear and eyes.

Yet Maxwell swore under oath that she had seen the young woman that same morning alive. Could this be a hideous hoax perpetrated by Jack the Ripper? Was it possible that Maxwell had conversed with the deadly assailant himself, clad in his victim's garments? Such ghoulish behavior was not beyond the realm of the killer who took Catherine Eddowes's kidney with him and boastingly claimed to have eaten one-half of it.

Inspector Frederick George Abberline of Scotland Yard offered his own testimony:

> I have heard the doctor's evidence and confirm what he says. I have taken an inventory of what was in the room. There had been a large fire, so large as to melt the spout off the kettle. I have since gone through the ashes in the grate & found nothing of consequence except that articles of womans clothing had been burnt which I presume was for the purpose of light as there was only one piece of candle in the room.[21]

What secrets lay embedded in the ashes? In this case, where there is smoke, there really is fire.

The strange testimony about Marie Jeanette Kelly's apparent return to life lingered in my mind. The coroner and jury believed that either Mrs. Maxwell had been wrong in her identification of Marie Kelly, or that she had mistaken as to the day on which she saw her. Inspector Abberline also doubted her statement at first, but later came to feel that Mrs. Maxwell's evidence needed more careful consideration.

Peter Underwood reported in his book an interesting theory of a citizen named John Morrison, who believed that James Kelly, Marie Jeanette Kelly's ex-husband, was Jack the Ripper. Mr. Morrison also proposed that Marie Kelly may have risen from the dead in order to expose her ex-husband to the authorities.

> Abberline went back to see her [Mrs. Maxwell] following the inquest. He tried time and again to get her to change her evidence but she stuck to her guns. Abberline went back to the Yard and said, in effect: That woman is telling the truth but I agree there must be some logical explanation. Could it be that the person responsible for these crimes is a woman? Did she kill Mary Kelly and then,

finding herself saturated with blood, change into Mary's clothes and leave the house? Anyone seeing her would think she was Mary.

His colleagues pointed out that even if this were the case what on earth was this Jill the Ripper doing flaunting herself in Dorset Street three to five hours after she had killed Mary? Could the reason that Mary appeared following her death be because she possessed knowledge unknown to any of the victims? She was the only victim to have heard the name Jack the Ripper and, among other things, the only one who could have identified James Kelly. Perhaps Mary appeared in the first instance to attract Mrs. Maxwell's attention; then perhaps she appeared outside The Britannia with James Kelly's image . . .[22]

There is another more intriguing explanation for Mrs. Maxwell's exchange with a "living Marie Kelly" on that fateful Friday morning, which will unfold later.

Among the items found in the charred remains of Kelly's room was a pipe that Kelly's boyfriend, Barnett, said was used by him. I found this to be crucial information. Barnett parted from Kelly on October 30 and did not see her again until November 9, the day she was killed. The pipe was left in the room to be found and displayed as police evidence.

The *Daily Telegraph* of November 13, 1888, quotes Inspector Abberline as saying: "There was a man's clay pipe in the room, and Barnett informed me he smoked it.[23]

My question was: Could it have belonged to somebody else who was Kelly's last visitor that night? Could it have belonged to the murderer?

1. Pamela West, *Yours Truly, Jack the Ripper, A Novel*, St. Martin's Press, New York, 1987.
2. *Daily Telegraph*, November 10, 1888.
3. Inquest Marie Jeanette Kelly, November 12, 1888.
4. *Daily Telegraph*, November 13, 1888.

5. Inquest Marie Jeanette Kelly, November 12, 1888.
6. *Daily Telegraph*, November 13, 1888.
7. Inquest Marie Jeanette Kelly, November 12, 1888.
8. *Ibid.*
9. *Ibid.*
10. *Daily Telegraph*, November 13, 1888.
11. Inquest Marie Jeanette Kelly, November 12, 1888.
12. *Ibid.*
13. *Ibid.*
14. *Ibid.*
15. *Ibid.*
16. *Ibid.*
17. *Daily Telegraph*, November 13, 1888.
18. *Ibid.*
19. Inquest Marie Jeanette Kelly, November 12, 1888.
20. *Daily Telegraph*, November 13, 1888.
21. Peter Underwood, *Jack the Ripper: One Hundred Years of Mystery*, Blandford Press, London, 1987, p. 135.
22. Inquest Marie Jeanette Kelly, November 12, 1888.
23. *Daily Telegraph*, November 13, 1888.

CHAPTER FIVE

More Than One

"A man was standing igniting a clay pipe . . ."

Witness's testimony at the
inquest on Elizabeth Stride,
October 29, 1888.

T HE WHITECHAPEL MURDERS were like scenes from a gripping
and bizarre horror story. The horrifying mutilations of Jack
the Ripper combine aspects of cannibalism with necrophiliac
behavior. Such misdirected hostility toward women is rooted, as
we know, in childhood experiences and relationships.[1] He may
have felt justified in establishing some sort of sexual rapport with a
prostitute, an encounter devoid of love. By some guise of charm or
gallantry, he was able to persuade the women to accede to his
demands. I would surmise that the sexual encounter was short and
abrupt, since the Ripper had only a few minutes to complete the
task of murder and mutilation and escape detection.

Utilizing all of the precepts of a skillful writer, the murderer
carefully set the scenario in a murky and desolate environment.
Secretiveness was his watchword. The drama was played out on
the streets of life instead of the pages of a book.

All of the victims were apparently strangled to prevent any
screaming for help. The Ripper also knew that strangulation
followed by a quick-drawn knife across the throat was an effective

74

method of avoiding being covered with the victim's blood. Perhaps the Ripper positioned himself behind his victims, feigning the onset of anal sex before he began his slaughter. What follows is a possible scenario of the Ripper and his victim.

The Ripper proposes his need to the victim. He offers her money, perhaps half a crown, to let him have sex from behind, anally. The woman accepts the generous offer and agrees. She is older and there were plenty of younger, more attractive girls to compete with. He had probably been embracing her, talking to her, and she could well have been happy to accept the proposal— better hurry up, she may have thought, before he changes his mind. She could even during those few moments have thought what she would buy with the money—maybe some gin, a decent bed for the night, the good jacket she had pawned that might now be redeemed.

Standing behind her, he swings his arm around her neck, squeezing as hard as he could, exerting this deadly pressure until she loses consciousness without being able to scream for help.

The victims were usually drunk and easily gave in to the persuasive man. But the killer also had to have a certain amount of muscular strength to overcome the women's struggles and to move the bodies about to carry out his mutilations.

Knowing that several prostitutes had been murdered in such a horrible fashion, why were these women still prepared to accept an unknown man's advances? Some of them harbored an unconscious attraction to the murderer who had been bold enough to kill some of their sisters and then disappear. Others merely incorporated the danger into their daily routine.

The crucial ingredient in the Whitechapel crimes was speed. The murderer would have to know the streets, the neighborhood, the buildings—to learn the quickest route to safety. David Berkowitz, the murderer known as Son of Sam, told me he spent many a night stalking his intended victims without being able to shoot them for fear of being discovered. He described what became an introductory ritual to his murders:

I did have a general idea of where I would be going in search of victims. So I familiarized myself with the streets and possible escape routes from those central areas. Also, I managed to learn all the streets by repeated trips into the area. I mean that there were nights in which I travelled all through a certain area but it turned unproductive. Naturally, I got to know streets by this method, too.[2]

To avoid arrest, Jack the Ripper learned to play out his murders in much the same way as Son of Sam did a hundred years later. Sam stalked his victims independently. Up until the death of Elizabeth Stride, I thought the Ripper did, too. Then on September 30, 1888, the Ripper was forced to flee in the middle of his murderous ritual because someone was coming. With a closer look at the details surrounding the Ripper murders, I was persuaded that the Whitechapel escapades involved an accomplice, a helper, who was posted to warn when somebody was approaching.

We know that the killer sent messages and letters offering clues to his identity. Emotionally disturbed murderers seldom kill if they cannot receive recognition for their acts. I was not convinced by the hoary premise that Jack the Ripper had crafted the perfect crime. Somewhere in the details of the murders lay the subtle clues of identification.

I began with the standard questions: When and where were the murders committed and how and why were they carried out? For more than a century, we have been told when and where the murders took place. More is yet to be learned about how the crimes were committed. But, little, if anything is known about the last question—Why? The latter is the most significant because it leads us directly to the rationale of the murder and of its perpetrator. In order to uncover the *why* of criminal behavior, we need first to identify the perpetrator.

To prove *who* was guilty of the Whitechapel murders, we have to find a suspect who was present at the scene of the crime and show that he had the opportunity, or created the opportunity, to commit the murder. We must also demonstrate the motive for the killing, either financial or emotional gain or revenge for having been humiliated or rejected, the need for such revenge being fueled further by inordinate feelings of hate or love.

The difficulty in ascertaining any murderer's identity can be overcome if we remember that, like the rest of us, every killer has individual psychobiosocial and emotional characteristics that mark his behavior. His style and method are the unique hallmarks of his work.

Jack the Ripper's cunning, methodical, goal-oriented and sophisticated execution of his victims and his swift disappearance from the murder scene indicate careful preparation. The subsequent frantic, almost feverish communications with the police authorities, the chairman of the Whitechapel Vigilante Committee, and the newspapers display the ambivalence of a man who was as eager to let himself be known as he was to keep his identity hidden.

. Each murder bore the obvious signs of a predator who enjoyed toying with his victims. The women were merely pawns, strategically moved about on his deadly chess board—before, during and after the attacks. It was a game in which only the winning player would remain alive.

The murderer, it appeared, enjoyed playing games. He was likely a sportsman. He played out his murders with resolve, defiantly, as if nothing would prevent him from achieving his goals, winner-take-all.

He was driven to kill; a force was compelling him, as though daring him to prove he could do it. Murder for the Ripper was the path to self-worth and emotional survival. As he searched out his victims, his defiance increased and finally exploded, resulting in a heap of desecrated bodies.

The personality of the killer was indelibly marked on each of his victims. I was convinced that the clue to his identity remained buried in the hulking mounds of investigative reports.

Each of the inquests, I was sure, offered further leads to his discovery.

On September 10, 1888, an inquiry was begun in the Alexandra Room of the Working Lads' Institute, Whitechapel Road, "respecting the death of Annie Chapman, who was found murdered in the backyard of 29, Hanbury-street, Spitalfields, on Saturday morning."[3] Officiating was Mr. Wynne E. Baxter, the Coroner for the North-Eastern Division of Middlesex, accompanied by Mr. George Collier, the Deputy Coroner.

Also attending were Detective-Inspectors Abberline (Scotland Yard), Helson and Chandler, and Detective-Sergeants Thicke and Leach who represented the Criminal Investigation Department and Commissioners of Police.

The Times (London) reported in its issue of September 11, 1888:

The courtroom was crowded, and, owing to the number of people assembled outside the building, the approaches had to be guarded by a number of police-constables . . .

John Davis, a carman, of 29, Hanbury-street, Spitalfields, deposed that he . . . was awake from 3 to about 5 o'clock, when he fell off to sleep for about half an hour. He got up about a quarter to 6. Soon afterwards he went across the yard . . . When he went into the yard on Saturday morning the back door was shut; but he was unable to say whether it was latched. The front door was wide open and he was not surprised at finding it so, as it was frequently left open all night. Between the yard of 29, Hanbury-street, and the next house there was a fence about 5 ft. high. When witness went down the steps he saw the deceased woman lying flat on her back . . .

Witness could see that her clothes were disarranged . . . Amelia Farmer stated that she lived at a common lodginghouse at 30, Dorset-street, Spitalfields, and had lived there for the past four years. She had identified the body of the deceased in the mortuary, and was sure it was that of Annie Chapman. The deceased formerly lived at Windsor, and was the widow of Frederick Chapman, a veterinary surgeon, who died about 18 months ago. For four years, or more, the deceased had lived apart from her husband, and during that period had principally resided in common lodginghouses in the neighborhoods of Whitechapel and Spitalfields. About two years since the deceased lived at 30, Dorset-street, and was then living with a man who made iron sieves.[4]

Another witness, James Kent, stated that the deceased had a handkerchief of some kind around her throat. Her face and hands were smeared with blood, as though she had been struggling. But further examination of the body showed no evidence of a struggle having taken place.

Rumors that Chapman was drunk when she was attacked were refuted in the coroner's report following her autopsy:

> The stomach contained a little food, but there was not any sign of fluid. There was no appearance of the deceased having taken alcohol, but there were signs of great deprivation, and he should say she had been badly fed. He was convinced she had not taken any strong alcohol for some hours before her death.[5]

The victim's face was swollen, and her tongue protruded, indicating she had suffocated. At one point during the inquest, a medical witness, Dr. George Bagster Phillips, clashed with the Coroner, Wynne E. Baxter, about whether all the details of the autopsy should be revealed. As a consequence and compromise, the court was cleared of all women and boys and "the witness proceeded to give medical and surgical evidence, totally unfit for publication, of the deliberate, successful, and apparently scientific manner in which the poor woman had been mutilated . . ."[6]

The Ripper murders have obvious sexual connotations. Not satisfied with having killed and desecrated Annie Chapman, he removed her vagina, bladder and intestines, all of which he placed on her right shoulder, and took her uterus away with him. At

Commercial Street

Metropolitan Police.

H Division.

14th September 1888

I beg to report having made enquiries at the Depot of the 1st Batt'n Sussex Regiment, North Camp, Farnborough 14th inst; the piece of envelope found near the body of deceased was identified by Capt Young Act'g Adjutant, as bearing the official stamp of the Regiment, and stated that the majority of the men used this paper which they purchased at the canteen. Enquiries were made amongst the men but none could be found who corresponded with anyone living at Spitalfields, or with any person whose address commencing with "S" The pay books were examined and no signature resembled the initials on the envelope. I made further enquiries at the Lynchford Road Post Office, and was informed by the proprietors Mess'rs Sumner & Thirkettle that the letter was posted there also that they had a large quantity of stock of the envelopes & paper in stock, and retailed them to any person.

J Chandler Insp't

Submitted 8th Neat Aug Sup'r

Ti Ch Supt Swanson 3.50 p

15.9.88

The September 14, 1888 report by Metropolitan Police Inspector Chandler, assigned to the investigation of Annie Chapman's murder.

forty-seven years old, she was the oldest of the victims, yet her body held attraction for this murderer.

The Times (London) reported the testimony of Amelia Richardson, the owner of 29 Hanbury Street, Spitalfields:

> About 6 o'clock on Saturday morning her grandson, Thomas Richardson, 14 years of age, who lived with her, went down stairs. They heard some one in the passage and thought the place was on fire. He returned directly afterwards, saying "Oh, grandmother, there is a woman murdered!" Witness went down immediately, and saw the body of deceased lying in the yard. [7]

One of the witnesses, John Pizer, a bootmaker, of 22 Mulberry Street, had been suspected of being the murderer of Annie Chapman. *The Times* (London) gave the following account of his testimony:

> He had been known by the nickname of "Leather Apron." He went home on Thursday night from the West-end of the town. He reached Mulberry-street about a quarter of 11 o'clock. His brother and stepmother also lived there. He remained indoors until he was arrested by Sergeant Thicke on Monday morning. Up to that time he had not left the house. His brother advised him to remain indoors as he was the object of a false suspicion. He did so in consequence of that. He was not now in custody and had cleared his character. [8]

Another important witness, Elizabeth Long, 138 Church Row, Whitechapel, was questioned. She was the wife of James Long, a park-keeper, and was the last one to see Annie Chapman alive. *The Times* (London) report of her testimony is as follows:

> On Saturday morning the 8th inst., she was passing down Hanbury-street from home and going to Spitalfields Market. It was about 5.30. She was certain of the time, as the brewers' clock had just

struck that time when she passed 29, Hanbury-street. Witness was on the right-hand side of the street—the same side as No. 29. She saw a man and woman on the pavement talking. The man's back was turned towards Brick-lane, while the woman's was towards the Spitalfields Market. They were talking together, and were close against the shutters of No. 29. Witness saw the woman's face. She had since seen the deceased in the mortuary, and was sure it was the face of the same person she saw in Hanbury-street. She did not see the man's face, except to notice that he was dark. He wore a brown deer-stalker hat, and she thought he had on a dark coat, but was not quite certain of that. She could not say what the age of the man was, but he looked to be over 40, and appeared to be a little taller than deceased. He appeared to be a foreigner, and had a shabby genteel appearance. Witness could hear them talking fondly, and she overheard him say to deceased, "Will you?" She replied, "Yes." They still stood there as witness passed, and she went onto her work without looking back. [9]

The Times gave an account of the testimony of a witness named Cadosh:

[I]t was about 5:20 when he was in the backyard of the adjoining house and heard a voice say "No," and three or four minutes afterwards a fall against the fence . . . [10]

The Coroner gave his summary of the events of the murder, along with reasons why no cries were heard from the victim.

He seized her by the chin. He pressed her throat, and while thus preventing the slightest cry, he at the same time produced insensibility and suffocation. There was no evidence of any struggle. The clothes were not torn. Even in those preliminaries, the wretch seems to have known how to carry out efficiently his nefarious work. The deceased was then lowered to the ground, and laid on her back: and although in doing so she may have fallen slightly against the fence, the movement was probably effected with care.

Her throat was then cut in two places with savage determination, and the injuries to the abdomen commenced. All was done with cool impudence and reckless daring; but perhaps nothing was more noticeable than the emptying of her pockets, and the arrangement of their contents with business-like precision in order near her feet. The murder seemed, like the Buck's-row case, to have been carried out without any cry. None of the occupants of the houses by which the spot was surrounded heard anything suspicious. The brute who committed the offence did not even take the trouble to cover up his ghastly work, but left the body exposed to the view of the first comer. That accorded but little with the trouble taken with the rings, and suggested either that he had at length been disturbed, or that, as daylight broke, a sudden fear suggested the danger of detection that he was running. There were two things missing. Her rings had been wrenched from her fingers and had not since been found, and the uterus had been taken from the abdomen.[11]

The murderer had apparently spent more time than he planned in the dissection of Annie Chapman, a salient point in the hypothesis that he was suddenly gripped by the fear of capture or discovery. Theories ranged from the possibility of someone approaching to the breaking of dawn to shed light on his grotesque handiwork.

Was there a companion standing guard during the attack who may have alerted the murderer? What caused the Ripper to leave so hurriedly after such careful surgical disembowelment?

The murderer knew that his dangerous work needed the cover of darkness. He also knew that there could be no delay in carrying out his plans. It was a *conditio sine qua non* that the murder conform to his emotional lust, and once done, that he disappear as soon as possible without being detected.

His sudden departure from his victim under threat of discovery undoubtedly left him unfulfilled by the attack on Annie Chapman. Therefore, it was not unreasonable to expect that other murders would follow. On the night of September 30, 1888, the murderer claimed two more victims, ravaging the bodies of Elizabeth Stride and Catherine Eddowes within three hours. Finally, about six weeks later, Marie Jeanette Kelly joined the list.

The Elizabeth Stride inquest commenced on October 2, 1888. At the outset, there was a great deal of confusion about the victim's identity. Hearings continued until October 26, 1888, at the Vestry Hall on Cable Street, St. George, in the East End, "respecting the death of Elizabeth Stride, who was found murdered in Berner Street, Aldgate, on the 30th ult."[12]

The Coroner's report presents a colorful picture of what occurred as the jury members tried to establish who the victim was. The Coroner explained:

The first difficulty which presented itself was the identification of the deceased. That was not an unimportant matter. Their trouble was principally occasioned by Mrs. Malcolm, who, after some hesitation, and after having had two further opportunities of viewing again the body, positively swore that the deceased was her sister—Mrs. Elizabeth Watts, of Bath. It had since been clearly proved that she was mistaken, notwithstanding the visions which were simultaneously vouchsafed at the hour of the death to her and her husband. If her evidence was correct, there were points of resemblance between the deceased and Elizabeth Watts which almost reminded one of the "Comedy of Errors." Both had been courted by policemen; they both bore the same Christian name, and were of the same age; both lived with sailors; both at one time kept coffee-houses at Poplar; both were nick-named "Long Liz"; both were said to have had children in charge of their husbands friends; both were given to drink; both lived in East-end common lodging-houses; both had been charged at the Thames Police-court; both had escaped punishment on the ground that they were subject to epileptic fits, although the friends of both were certain that this was a fraud; both had lost their front teeth, and both had been leading very questionable lives. Whatever might be the true explanation of this marvelous similarity, it appeared to be pretty satisfac-

84

torily proved that the deceased was Elizabeth Stride, and that about the year 1869 she was married to a carpenter named John Thomas Stride. Unlike the other victims in the series of crimes in this neighbourhood—a district teeming with representatives of all nations—she was not an Englishwoman. [13]

The Coroner continued:

. . . the victim was born in Sweden in the year 1843, and had resided in the country for upwards of twenty years . . . She was last seen alive by Kidney in Commercial-street on the evening of Tuesday, September 25. She was sober, but never returned home that night. She alleged that she had some words with her paramour, but this he denied. The next day she called during his absence, and took away some things, but, with this exception, they did not know what became of her until the following Thursday, when she made her appearance at her old quarters in Flower and Dean-street. Here she remained until Saturday, September 29. On that day she cleaned the deputy's rooms, and received a small remuneration for her trouble. Between 6 and 7 o'clock on that evening she was in the kitchen wearing the jacket, bonnet, and striped silk neckerchief which were afterwards found on her. She had at least 6d. in her possession, which was possibly spent during the evening. Before leaving she gave a piece of velvet to a friend to take care of until her return, but she said neither where she was going nor when she would return. She had not paid for her lodgings, although she was in a position to do so. They knew nothing of her movements during the next four or five hours at least—possibly not till the finding of her lifeless body. But three witnesses spoke to having seen a woman that they identified as the deceased with more or less certainty, and at times within an hour and a quarter of the period when, and at places within 100 yards of the spot where she was ultimately found. [14]

Excerpts from the testimony of the witness William Marshall follow:

I live at 64, Berner-street, Commercial-road, and am a labourer. On Sunday last I saw the body of deceased in the mortuary. I recognize it as that of a woman I saw on Saturday evening . . . That was about a quarter to 12 . . . She was standing talking to a man . . .

The Coroner.—Was she wearing a flower when you saw her?— No . . .

The Coroner.—What sort of cap was he wearing?—A round cap with a small peak to it; something like what a sailor would wear.

The Coroner.—What height was he?—About 5 ft. 6 in., and he was rather stout. He was decently dressed, and I should say he worked at some light business, and had more the appearance of a clerk than anything else.

The Coroner.—Did you see whether he had any whiskers?— From what I saw of his face I do not think he had . . .

The Coroner.—What sort of a coat was it?—A cutaway one.

The Coroner.—You are quite sure this is the woman?—Yes, I am. I did not take much notice of them. I was standing at my door, and what attracted my attention first was her standing there some time, and he was kissing her. I heard the man say to deceased, You would say anything but your prayers. [15]

Marshall described the man he saw as one who "was mild speaking and appeared to be an educated man . . ." [16]

Another witness, James Brown, testified:

As I passed them I heard the woman say, "No, not to-night, some other night." . . . I should say the man was about 5 ft. 7 in. in height . . . [17]

Police constable William Smith reported that the man he saw with Elizabeth Stride had a "respectable appearance." He said:

He was about 5 ft. 7 in. as near as I could say. He had on a hard felt deerstalker hat of dark colour and dark clothes . . . He wore dark trousers . . . I did not see much of the face of the man except that he had no whiskers. [18]

Based upon the facts and observations reported by the witnesses, we may conclude that the deceased was in the company of a man for at least one hour before she was killed, and that about fifteen minutes before she was found dead, she refused the advances of her companion. Was it, as the Coroner posited, the same man who was seen with the victim on three different occasions by different witnesses? Could there have been more than one man involved in carrying out the murder of Elizabeth Stride?

The reports by the Metropolitan Police concerning the murder of Stride further clarified the number of men seen with the victim. On October 19, 1888, the diligent Donald S. Swanson, Chief Inspector of the Metropolitan Police, Criminal Investigation Department, recorded the number of persons who were present at the murder scene:

12.35 A.M. 30th. City Policeman 452 Smith saw a man and a woman, the latter with a red rose, talking in Berner-street. This policeman on seeing the body identified it as being that of the woman whom he had seen. He thus describes the man as, age 28, height 5 ft. 7 in., complexion dark, *small dark moustache* [author's emphasis], dress dark diagonal coat, hard felt hat, white collar and tie.

12.45 A.M. 30th. Israel Schwartz of 22 Helen-street (*Document 150*) Backchurch Lane stated that at that hour on turning into Berner-street from Commercial Road had got as far as the gateway where the murder was committed, he saw a man stop to speak to a woman who was standing in the gateway. The man tried to pull the woman into the street, he turned her around and threw her down on the footway and the woman screamed three times, but not very loudly.

On crossing to the opposite side of the street, he saw a second man standing *lighting his pipe* [author's emphasis]. The man who threw the woman down called out apparently to the man on the opposite side of the road, "Lipski," and then Schwartz walked away, but finding that he was followed by the second man he ran as far as the railway arch but the man did not follow so far.[19]

Swanson wrote in the margin of his report:

The use of "Lipski" increased my belief that the murderer was a
Jew. [20]

The bizarre murders magnified the prejudice of many people
who preferred to believe that the perpetrator of the crimes was a
Jew. At first, it seemed that the bias was founded in fact, but the
accusations against Jewish suspects eventually proved false.

Later, we will discover why the name "Lipski" was used and its
significance in the murders.

Chief Swanson's report continued:

Schwartz cannot say whether the two men were together or known
to each other. (*Document 151*) Upon being taken to the Mortuary,
Schwartz identified the body as that of the woman he had seen and
he thus describes the first man who threw the woman down: age
about 30, height 5 ft. 5 in., complexion fair, hair dark, small brown
moustache, full face, broad shouldered, dress dark jacket and trousers, black cap with peak, had nothing in his hands. Second man:
age 35, height 5 ft. 11 in., complexion fair, hair light brown,
moustache brown, dress dark overcoat, old black hard felt hat wide
brim, had a *clay* pipe in his *hand* . . . [author's emphasis]

The description of the man seen by the policeman was circulated
amongst the police by wire and by authority of Commissioner, it
was also given to the press. On the evening of 30th the man
Schwartz gave the description of the man he had seen ten minutes
later than the City Police and it was circulated by wire. It will be
observed that allowing for differences of opinion between the City
Police and Schwartz as to apparent age and height of the man each
saw with the woman whose body they both identified, there are
serious differences in the description of dress:—thus the City Police
describes the dress of the man whom he saw as black diagonal coat,
hard felt hat, while Schwartz describes the dress of the man he saw
as dark jacket, black cap with peak, so that at least it is rendered
doubtful whether they are describing the same man.

If Schwartz is to be believed, (*Document 153*) and the Police report of his statement casts no doubt upon it, it follows if they are describing different men that the man Schwartz saw and described is the more probable of the two to be the murderer, for a quarter of an hour afterwards the body is found murdered. At the same time, account must be taken of the fact that the throat only of the victim was cut in this instance which measured by time, considering meeting (if with a man other than Schwartz saw) the time for the agreement, the murderous action would I think be a question of so many minutes, five at least, ten at most, so that I respectfully submit it is not clearly proved that the man that Schwartz saw is the murderer although it is clearly the more probable of the two.[21]

In the margin of *Document 153* is written a long comment ending with "The Police officially do not contest the 2nd man whom Schwartz saw on the other side of the street and who followed Schwartz."[22]

It is easy to understand the confusion experienced by the inquest members when the witness Schwartz reported he had seen two persons at the site of the murder. Naturally, the police authorities were bewildered at the two different descriptions of the person seen in the area.

The long-established and widely held opinion is that there was only one Jack the Ripper. But the circumstances surrounding the murder of Elizabeth Stride contain a distinguishing variable that suggests otherwise. Her mutilation seemed to have been interrupted, and indeed it was. In other words, the murderer was warned by an accomplice.

An extraordinary force of policemen was constantly on patrol to monitor the movements of all suspects. In addition to the police presence, private citizens were on the alert. The dragnet was believed too tight to escape. But no one had contemplated that the Ripper had a helper.

The testimony at the inquest of Elizabeth Stride was revealing, but it passed unnoticed by the beleaguered jury. Two men were seen together near the scene, but the inquest members did not connect their presence. When I read the information concerning two men at the murder scene, it came as a confirmation rather than a surprise. My intensive studies of the facts already had indicated that the Ripper murders were the work of a criminal partnership.

Disagreement continued among the authorities over whether two persons were involved at the murder scene. Three witnesses reported what appeared at first to be similar descriptions. But later reports of their testimony noted certain discrepancies in their descriptions. The controversial descriptions were summarized in *The Times* (London) of October 26, 1888:

> With regard to the man seen, there were many points of similarity, but some of dissimilarity, in the descriptions of the three witnesses; but these discrepancies did not conclusively prove that there was more than one man in the company of the deceased, for every day's experience showed how facts were differently observed and differently described by honest and intelligent witnesses. Brown, who saw least in consequence of the darkness of the spot at which the two were standing, agreed with Smith that his clothes were dark and that his height was about 5 ft. 7 in., but he appeared to him to be wearing an overcoat nearly down to his heels; while the description of Marshall accorded with that of Smith in every respect but two. They agreed that he was respectably dressed in a black cut away coat and dark trousers, and that he was of middle age and without whiskers. On the other hand, they differed with regard to what he was wearing on his head. Smith stated he wore a hard felt deer stalker of dark colour; Marshall that he was wearing a round cap with small peak like a sailor's. [23]

An earlier issue of *The Times* (London) reported on October 19, 1888, what Chief Inspector Swanson described as one of the men seen with Catherine Eddowes:

> Before concluding in dealing with these two descriptions, the descriptions of these two men, I venture to insert here for the purpose

of comparison with these two descriptions, the description of a man seen with a woman in Church Passage close to Mitre Square at 1.35 A.M. by two men coming out of a club close by:—age 30, height 5 ft., 7 or 8 in., complexion fair, fair moustache, medium build, dress pepper and salt colour loose jacket, grey cloth cap with peak of same colour, reddish handkerchief tied in a knot round neck, appearance of a sailor. In this case I understand from the City Police that Mr. Lewin, one of the men, identified the clothes only of the murdered woman, Eddowes, which is a serious drawback to the value of the description of the man ten minutes afterwards. The body is found horribly mutilated and it is therefore reasonable to believe that the man he saw was the murderer, but for purposes of comparison this description is nearer to that given by Schwartz than to that given by the City Police.[24]

Police investigation was painstaking and resolute. No detail was overlooked; every avenue was explored.

Chief Inspector Swanson reported:

Under head by the Police 80,000 pamphlets to occupiers were issued and a house to house enquiry made not only involving the result of enquiries from the occupiers but also a search by Police and with a few exceptions—but not such as to convey suspicions— covered the area bounded by the City Police boundary on the one hand, Lavel-street, Commercial-street, Great Eastern Railway and Boston-street, then by Albert-street, Duck-street, Chicksand- street and Great Garden-street to Whitechapel Road, then to the City boundary. Under this head also, Common Lodging Houses were visited and over 2,000 Lodgers were examined.[25]

Chief Inspector Swanson's account of the diligent efforts of the police continued as follows:

. . . enquiry was also made by Thames Police as to sailors on board ships in docks or river and extended enquiry as to Asiatics present in London. About 80 persons have been detained at the different police stations in the Metropolis and their statements taken and verified by police. Enquiry has been made into the movements of a number of persons estimated at upwards of 300 respecting what communications were received by police and such enquiries are continued. Seventy-six butchers and slaughterers have been visited and the characters of the men employed enquired into, this embraces all servants who had been employed for the past six months. . . . Up to date, although the number of letters daily is considerably lessened, the other enquiries respecting alleged suspicious persons continues as numerous.

There are now 994 dockets besides police reports.

(Signed) Donald S. Swanson
Chief Inspector[26]

Despite such far-reaching and thorough inquiry, Catherine Eddowes would not escape her deadly fate. However, postmortem examinations of the body offered no avenues of enlightenment about the killer's identity.

It was equally difficult to locate members of the victim's family. As reported in *The Times* (London) of October 12, 1888, Detective Sergeant John Mitchell said:

I have made every enquiry to find the Father and Brother of the last Witness without success. I have found a Paramour named Conway but he is not the man. I with other officers have used every endeavor and enquiry possible to be made with a view to trace the murderer.

(Signed) John Mitchell[27]

The inquest began October 4, 1888, at the mortuary in Goldenlane, to investigate the death of Catherine Eddowes, who was found murdered in Mitre Square on September 30, 1888. Mr. Crawford stated at the opening of the proceedings that "he was present as representing the City Police, for the purpose of rendering the Coroner and the jury every possible assistance. If, when the witnesses were giving evidence, he thought it desirable to put any question, probably he would have the Coroner's permission to do so." The Coroner confirmed Mr. Crawford's presumption in answering, "By all means."[28]

The City Solicitor Crawford, acting as legal counsel for the City Police, controlled and directed the Eddowes inquest. Several times, Mr. Crawford interrupted testimony or diverted the proceedings to interject his own theories and opinions.

Testimony was given by Dr. Frederick Gordon Brown, 17 Finsbury Circus, a surgeon with the London City Police, who stated that the murderer "had a good deal of knowledge as to the position of the organs in the abdominal cavity and the way of removing them . . ."[29] But Dr. George William Sequeria, another surgeon, disagreed. He believed that the perpetrator lacked any significant anatomical knowledge.

Dr. Brown speculated that the victim was mutilated after her death. When asked by Mr. Crawford to explain the reason why her face had been marred, the doctor responded simply, "to disfigure the corpse."[30]

The Metropolitan Police report of November 6, 1888, indicated that studies of the mutilation had so far given no evidence of "anatomical knowledge in the sense that it evidenced the hand of a qualified surgeon, so that the Police could narrow their enquiries into certain classes of persons. On the other hand as in the Metropolitan Police cases, the medical evidence shewed [sic] that the murder could have been committed by a person who had been a hunter, a butcher, a slaughterman, as well as a student in surgery or a properly qualified surgeon."[31]

The news of Catherine Eddowes's murder "at once was telegraphed to headquarters and Inspector Edward Gollard dispatched a constable to Dr. Gordon Brown and proceeded to Mitre Square, arriving there 2-3 minutes past 2. I found Dr. Sequeria and several police officers at the dead person lying in the South West corner of the Square . . . I took immediate steps to have the neighbourhood searched for the person who had committed the crime."

Mr. MacWilliam, chief of the Detective Department, on his arrival shortly after with a number of Detectives, sent to have immediate search and in lodging houses several men were stopped and searched without any good result. I have had a house-to-house enquiry in the vicinity of Mitre-Square but I failed to find anything excepting the witnesses to be produced named Lawende and Levy.[32]

It was estimated that the murderer took the life of Eddowes in no more than five minutes. That was enough time to be detected. But despite the intensive police search, the murderer was able to avoid the police net.

A portion of the apron worn by the victim was produced at the inquest, along with a matching portion that was picked up in Goulston Street shortly after the murder. The evidence helped to define the route the murderer had taken and the swiftness of his movements. I again reflected on the rapid disappearance and whether it may have been facilitated by an accomplice acting as sentinel during the bloody onslaught.

The body was mutilated after being positioned on the ground. Imagine how difficult it would be for one man to strangle the victim into unconsciousness, then cut her throat, then lay her down on the ground, and finally begin his surgical design on her abdomen—all without anyone noticing a single step of the grue-some activity. Notwithstanding the darkness of night, some peo-ple were moving about. The Ripper certainly did so—scurrying from the deadly spot in Mitre Square in search of a public sink in the street where he could wash off the victim's blood.

Following the murders of Stride and Eddowes, the atmosphere in the neighborhood was electric. Rumors about likely suspects flew around the area. Some witnesses came forth, but their testi-mony was short-circuited and they were hurried through the pro-ceedings. On certain occasions, witnesses were deliberately prevented from giving a full description of the person seen at the murder scene.

At the inquest on Catherine Eddowes, hindrances to exposing a possible suspect were particularly blatant. *The Times* (London) of October 12, 1888 reported:

Joseph Lawende said that he lived at 45 Norfolk-road, Dalston. He was a commercial traveller. On the night of the murder he was at the Imperial Club in Duke-street, with Joseph Levy and Harry Harris. They went out of the club at half-past 1, and left the place about five minutes later. They saw a man and a woman standing together at a corner in Church-passage, in Duke-street, which led into Mitre-square. The woman was standing with her face towards the man. Witness could not see the woman's face; the man was taller than she. She had on a black jacket and bonnet. He saw her put her hand on the man's chest. Witness had seen some clothing at the police-station, and he believed the articles were the same that the woman he referred to was wearing.

The Coroner.—Can you tell us what sort of man it was with whom she was speaking?—(Answer) He had on a cloth cap with a peak. [33]

The Eddowes inquest report elaborated on Joseph Lawende's account:

Joseph Lawende, 45 Norfolk Road, Dalston, Commercial Traveller, being sworn saith—On the night of the 29th I was at the Imperial Club. Mr. Joseph Levy and Mr. Harry Harris were with me. It was raining. We left there to go out at ½ past one and we left the house about 6 minutes later. I walked awhile further from the others standing in the corner of Church Passage in Duke Street which leads to Mitre Square. I saw a woman. She was standing with her face towards a man. I only saw her back. She had her hand on his chest. The man was taller than she was. She had a black jacket and a black bonnet. I have seen the articles which it was stated belonged to her at the police station. My belief is that they were the same clothes which I had seen upon the deceased. She appeared to me short. The man had a cloth cap on with a cloth peak. I have given a description of the man to the police. I doubt whether I should know him again. [34]

At that point in the interview, *The Times* (London) reported that Mr. Crawford interrupted:

> Unless the jury wish it I have a special reason why no further description of this man be given now.
>   The jury assented to Mr. Crawford's wish.
>   The Coroner.—You have given a description of the man to the police, I suppose?—(Answer) Yes.
>   The Coroner.—Would you know him again?—(Answer) I doubt it.[35]

Crawford's interruption, as reported in *The Times* (London), appeared nowhere in the actual report of the inquest. We see that, following a minimal description of his cloth cap, further dialogue on the suspect was stifled. It was clear that certain information was being withheld from the public. Someone had to be protected.

Why did the solicitor for the City Police suppress Lawende's description of the man he witnessed at the place of murder? Did the police fear that such public knowledge would hamper the investigations? It seems unlikely.

The description withheld at the inquest on Catherine Eddowes surfaced in 1966 in a *London Hospital Gazette* article entitled "More about Jack the Ripper." It was written by Professor Francis E. Camps, M.D., M.R.C.P., F.C. Path., a respected pathologist, who reported the suspect "as a man about 30 years, 5 ft. 9 in. in height, with a small fair moustache, dressed in something like navy serge and with a deer stalker's hat, peak fore and aft."[36] Professor Camps also noted that the man seen with Eddowes wore a red handkerchief around his neck.[37]

The inquest jury rendered its verdict with not one comment on the persons seen at the murder site. They merely stated that Catherine Eddowes was willfully murdered. The killer was still at large and unknown.

1. William T. Eckert, "The Whitechapel Murders. The Case of Jack the Ripper," *The American Journal of Forensic Medicine and Pathology*, Vol. 2, No. 1, March, 1981, pp. 53–60.
2. David Abrahamsen, M.D., *Confessions of Son of Sam*, Columbia University Press, New York, 1985, pp. 93–94.
3. *The Times* (London), September 11, 1888.
4. *Ibid.*
5. Report by Joseph Chandler, Murder of Annie Chapman, Metropolitan Police, September 15, 1888.
6. *Ibid.*
7. *The Times* (London), September 11, 1888.
8. *Ibid.*, September 14, 1888.
9. *Ibid.*, September 20, 1888.
10. *Ibid.*, September 27, 1888.
11. *Ibid.*, September 20, 1888.
12. *Ibid.*, October 26, 1888.
13. *Ibid.*
14. *Ibid.*
15. *Ibid.*
16. *Ibid.*
17. *Ibid.*
18. *Ibid.*
19. *Ibid.*
20. Report by Donald S. Swanson, Chief Inspector, Murder of Elizabeth Stride, Metropolitan Police, October 19, 1888.
21. *Ibid.*
22. *Ibid.*
23. *The Times* (London), October 26, 1888.
23. *Ibid.*, October 19, 1888.
24. Report by Donald S. Swanson, Chief Inspector, Murder of Elizabeth Stride, Metropolitan Police, October 19, 1888.
25. *Ibid.*
26. *The Times* (London), October 12, 1888.
27. *Ibid.*, October 5, 1888.
28. *Coroner's Inquest: Catherine Eddowes*, No. 135, 1888, p. 1.
29. *Ibid.*

30. *Ibid.*, pp. 20–21.
31. Report of Metropolitan Police, Murder of Catherine Eddowes, November 6, 1888.
32. *Ibid.*
33. *The Times* (London), October 12, 1888.
34. *Coroner's Inquest: Catherine Eddowes*, No. 135, 1888, pp. 35–36.
35. *The Times* (London), October 12, 1888.
36. Report by Professor Francis E. Camps, *London Hospital Gazette*, Vol. LXIX, No. 1, April, 1966.
37. *Ibid.*

PART THREE

ILLNESS AND MISERY START AT HOME

CHAPTER SIX

Encounter at Eton

"A life unexamined is not worth living."

PLATO,
The Apology

I N ORDER TO prove a person guilty of a murder, we must show that he was present at the scene of the crime. Two people have emerged who were present at the murders that claimed the lives of Elizabeth Stride and Catherine Eddowes. A third murder involving the two will be re-examined once the murderers' identities are revealed. We will explore the possible emotional connection of these perpetrators and whether each had the state of mind to carry out these horrendous rituals.

It is obvious that such murderous men harbor within themselves a violent rage that subsides, at least temporarily, only after it has found expression. In the course of extensive research and working experience, I have found that certain people exhibit strong tendencies toward violent and murderous behavior. Given the right stimuli, one may move along the criminal continuum from an enraged person to a homicidal maniac.

Murderers generally share one common characteristic—intense personal torment. The turmoil is often not apparent on the surface, but inside they feel trapped, doomed to a never-ending battle between their sexual drives and the dominance of family or social

101

pressures. Any one of these self-repressive situations could trigger murderous impulses.

We know that inner conflicts in adults are often due to a serious traumatic experience in early childhood—perhaps, before the child is one or two years old. The child learns quickly to quash his hateful emotions, but the feelings accumulate throughout his development.

The more extensive the pressure, the more helpless and impotent he feels. Overwhelmed by his frustration, he is subject to angry and hostile outbursts, and in severe circumstances, will retaliate to avenge his feelings of insignificance and castration.

British culture applauded propriety and self-restraint. The combination of a repressive societal climate and maternal or paternal deprivation or domination creates an explosive environment for a potential assassin.

At the time of the Whitechapel murders, Britain had reached the apex of military, financial and colonial prominence. We can imagine, therefore, the national humiliation that the Ripper murders caused throughout a land accustomed to considering itself the hub of civilization. For a brief historical period, the image of the British Empire as the paradigm of human achievement had succumbed to fear and barbarism.

Many English people were unnerved by the influx of foreigners and by their unfamiliar manners. So it seemed quite natural for the authorities to turn their attention to the foreigners who had settled in Whitechapel. Who else but a foreigner would commit such unspeakable acts of murder? Certainly not a "terribly civilized" Englishman!

Whitechapel had become an enclave for Jews emigrating from eastern as well as western Europe. Their meager and impoverished existence was made even more oppressive by the prejudice against them demonstrated by a substantial core of the population. The Jews felt threatened by the police, who in turn were being pressed by higher authorities to find the Whitechapel killer. The community residents lived in fear of attack and accusation. The police lived in fear of faltering in their reputation as well as in their protection of the public.

The roster of suspects kept growing. Important names joined the ranks, among them Alexander Pedechenco, a secret Czarist agent, and even Grigory Rasputin, who would become a notorious figure during the reign of Czar Nicholas II. Also named was Jack Pizer, one of the Jewish immigrants, who was actually arrested and jailed for a short time.

Dr. Thomas Neill Cream was another suspect. He was later charged with killing four London prostitutes in 1891 and executed for these crimes on November 15, 1892. During the time of the Ripper murders, however, he was incarcerated in Joliet Prison in Illinois, not returning to England until 1891.

Another name bandied about was Prince Albert Victor Edward (or Prince Eddy, as he was known to his family), the oldest son of the Prince of Wales and the presumptive heir to Queen Victoria's throne. Being in the public eye always attracted attention. Of course, the prince's cavorting with suspected homosexual groups (which included his strong attachment to J. K. Stephen) and his patronizing of male brothels did not quell the spreading gossip of his possible involvement in the murders.

The prince, later entitled Duke of Clarence and Avondale, was never formally questioned. On one occasion, Prince Eddy was rounded up during a raid at a male brothel on Cleveland Street, but, unlike the others, he was released immediately. There were spurts of rumors that the royal family's physician, Sir William Gull, M.D., of London, had intervened to protect the prince. Gull was physician to Queen Victoria from 1872 to 1890, and during that time he also attended the Prince of Wales as well as his son, Prince Eddy.

More specific implication of Prince Eddy had to await this century, with an article in *The Criminologist* of November 1970, by Dr. Thomas E. A. Stowell, a distinguished physician.[1] Dr.

Stowell died shortly after his article was published and his hypothesis was never fully investigated.

Michael Harrison, in his investigative rendition of the murders, originally suspected Prince Eddy. Later, he altered his opinion and designated as the culprit James Kenneth Stephen, a graduate of Eton and Cambridge, who had been the prince's tutor at Cambridge.[2] Harrison painted a clear picture of the historical background, but his theories lacked psychological insight.

Donald Rumbelow, a policeman and enthusiast on the subject of Jack the Ripper, has become a prolific writer about the unsolved murders. In his view, "while he [J.K. Stephen] certainly is one of the likeliest suspects yet, on the other hand, there is once again no evidence whatsoever."[3] I find this conclusion of a dearth of evidence entirely incorrect. The situation was, in fact, rich in undeciphered hidden clues left by the killer.

Harrison provided us with a careful scrutiny of the social conditions of the era, but he could not discern the emotional elements of his subject. Rumbelow had been trained in investigating the format of the crime, and not the conduct of the criminal. To unveil a perpetrator of such extreme criminal behavior, it is essential to delve beyond the facts and circumstances into the psyche of the suspect.

It is an analysis of the psychological parameters that enabled me to discover that the Ripper murders were perpetrated by Prince Eddy and J. K. Stephen. That realization came years after wading through the police compilation of misanthropes.

One of the most popular suspects was Montague John Druitt, who was found drowned in the Thames at the end of 1888. It is he who Martin Howells and Keith Skinner believe was the Ripper. In their book, *The Ripper Legacy: The Life and Death of Jack the Ripper*, they include some of the details of the inquest on Druitt's body:

Unfortunately, the official report of the proceedings has not survived, which has meant that we had to rely on the good offices of three newspapers. As the inquest was held in Chiswick, where the body was found, the proceedings were covered most thoroughly by the *Acton, Chiswick and Turnham Green Gazette* on Saturday, 5 January 1889:

Found Drowned.

Shortly after mid-day on Monday, a waterman named Winslade of Chiswick found the body of a man, well dressed, floating in the Thames off Thorneycroft's. He at once informed a constable, and without delay the body was conveyed on the ambulance to the mortuary. On Wednesday afternoon, Dr. Diplock, coroner, held the inquest at the Lamb Tap, when the following evidence was adduced:

William H. Druitt said that he lived at Bournemouth, and that he was a solicitor. The deceased was his brother, who was 31 last birthday. He was a barrister-at-law and an assistant master in a school at Blackheath. He had stayed with witness at Bournemouth for a night towards the end of October. Witness heard from a friend on the 11th of December that deceased had not been heard of at his chambers for more than a week. Witness then went to London to make inquiries, and at Blackheath he found that deceased had got into serious trouble at the school, and had been dismissed. That was on the 30th of December. Witness had deceased's things searched where he resided, and found a paper addressed to him (produced). The Coroner read the letter, which was to this effect: "Since Friday I felt I was going to be like mother [i.e., become insane] and the best thing for me was to die."[4]

Further information on Montague John Druitt revealed that he had taken the Blackheath private school position because he was doing poorly as a barrister. He was also homosexual and may have been sexually involved with some of the boys at the school. Certainly, his dismissal was swift and unceremonious. The official cause of his death was suicide. But Howells and Skinner noted in their book that Druitt had purchased a return ticket from Chiswick, which would seem to indicate that he had in mind a return to London.

If Druitt's demise was not by his own hand, then the possibility exists that he was murdered. The large stones found in his trouser pockets could have been placed there by someone who intended to simulate the suicidal death of the person who could have been the distraught Whitechapel murderer. In that way, the true culprit would evade justice.

The Druitt case is a rather convoluted story, but I will summarize the facts that have made him a suspect in the Jack the Ripper murders.

It appears that Druitt was acquainted with Harry Stephen, J. K. Stephen's younger brother. To quote Howells and Skinner again:

> Most significant of all was the unavoidable fact that Harry Lushington Stephen, the brother of J. K. Stephen, had chambers at No. 3 King's Bench Walk, just three doors away from Druitt at No. 9. J. K. himself was at Lincoln's Inn, while Herbert Stephen, J. K.'s other brother, was immediately opposite King's Bench Walk, at No. 4 Paper Buildings. The more Knight [Stephen Knight, the author of "Jack the Ripper: The Final Solution," published in *The Criminologist*, November 1976] looks at Druitt, the more he realizes that he is surrounded by people who were, or who have become, associated with the Whitechapel murders. At No. 9 King's Bench Walk itself, on the floor below Druitt, was fellow Wykehamist [the English term for men educated at Winchester, the outstanding boys' school founded by a medieval Archbishop of Canterbury named William of Wykeham] Reginald Brodie Dyke Acland, the brother of Sir William Gull's son-in-law. Also here was the solicitor Edward Henslowe Bedford, who one year after the Ripper murders would be deeply involved in covering up the Cleveland Street scandal, in which certain aristocratic and influential homosexuals, including Clarence, were narrowly to avoid public shame and ruin.[5]

Druitt's association with Harry Stephen may well have brought him into contact with J. K. Stephen and Prince Eddy. In fact, Howells and Skinner found an explanation for the confusion that

Montague John Druitt, a failed barrister and schoolteacher, was found drowned in the Thames river within weeks after the last Jack the Ripper murder.

led to the involvement of Prince Eddy as a suspect. The authors claimed that "it is quite possible that the Prince could indeed have fallen under suspicion, for Clarence and Druitt were remarkably alike in physical appearance."[6]

They continue: "The two photographs commonly used to demonstrate this likeness are startling enough, but the later photograph of Druitt (reproduced in this book for the first time) clearly shows him sporting a moustache which would have made the resemblance even more dramatic."[7]

The comparison of the photographs has a major flaw. Terence Sharkey in his book about Jack the Ripper, *100 Years of Investigation: The Facts, The Fiction, The Solution*, commented on a photograph of Druitt: "A contemporary photograph shows only a clean-shaven Druitt, but it was taken at Winchester a dozen or more years before the crimes."[8]

Assuming the picture was taken in 1876, Prince Eddy would have been only twelve years old. When we consider the age difference between them, it seems unlikely that Druitt, twelve years later, would be mistaken for the younger Prince Eddy.

The police also suspected men with medical backgrounds, on account of the skill with which the knife was wielded. At one point, the Home Office inquired about "three insane medical students." A *schochet* (a Jewish ritual slaughterer of cows and chickens) was also implicated by this theory.

Even a woman was suspected, by no less an authority than Sir Arthur Conan Doyle, creator of the master sleuth Sherlock Holmes, who suggested the murders were committed by a psychotic midwife. Though this theory was quickly dismissed, it made me think that the Whitechapel murderer might well have been a man dressed as a woman. This would not be unusual if the murderer were a homosexual.

The important question still remains. What were the possible motivations that might have led not one, but two men to undertake these crimes. And why, in view of the clear descriptions offered by witnesses, were they never apprehended?

At least two witnesses gave many details of men they saw near the murder scenes. I perused countless reports from the Chief of Police during my research, but found no concrete information that the police acted in any way to locate these men.

Members of the jury at the inquest on Elizabeth Stride were particularly informed of the descriptions of men witnessed at the murder scene. Why did the inquest lawyers and the police authorities gloss over the descriptive details in the testimony? Surely, the jury must have experienced personal conflict in disregarding what they learned from the witness Schwartz and then failing to investigate further.

It is possible that prejudice intervened. Schwartz was a foreigner; he was also Jewish. He did not speak the Queen's English. Perhaps, in the context of a formal British inquiry, he could not, or would not, be taken seriously. The innuendoes recur throughout the Ripper investigations. I remind you of the remarks made by Chief Inspector Swanson during the investigation of Elizabeth Stride's murder: "The use of 'Lipski' increased my belief that the murderer was a Jew."[9]

The Chief Inspector reflected the prevailing anti-Semitic viewpoint of the population. The panic felt by the citizens and the pressure on the police were naturally conducive to creating a scapegoat. History has consistently shown that people faced with danger seek out a sacrifice, like a primitive ritual, to allay their fears and practice their prejudices. Anti-Semitism, like any prejudice, is rooted in ignorance rather than in hate, and ignorance is a defect against which even the gods fight in vain.

In one of the reports of the inquest proceedings on Elizabeth Stride, dated November 1, 1888, Superintendent Abberline explained that "Lipski" was a Jewish man who was hanged in 1884 for murdering a Jewish woman.[10] Thereafter, the name Lipski, according to the Superintendent, came to be used generally as a derogatory term for the Jewish immigrant. Abberline suggested that one of the perpetrators of the Ripper murders, "apparently ill-using the deceased woman," directed the insult toward Schwartz, who had witnessed two men at the scene of the murder shortly before it occurred.

Further explication of the name "Lipski" is extracted from a memo from the Office of the Home Secretary:

A statement has been made by a man named Schwartz to the effect that he had heard a person who was pulling about a woman identified as Elizabeth Stride 15 minutes before the murder off Berner Street took place, call out "Lipki" [sic] to an individual who was on the opposite side of the road. It does not appear whether the man used the word "Lipski" as a mere ejaculation meaning in mockery, I am going to "Lipski" the woman, or whether he was calling to a man across the road by his proper name. In the latter case, assuming that the man using the word was the murderer, the murderer must have an acquaintance in Whitechapel named Lipski.

Mr. Matthews presumes that this clue has been one of the suggestions with regard to which searching enquiries have been made: although no tangible results have been obtained as regards the detection of the murderer; but he will be glad if he can be furnished with a report as to any investigations made to trace the man Lipski. [11]

Another letter, marked Confidential and dated November 6, 1888, from Sir Charles Warren to the Home Office, stated that "the name 'Lipski,' which he [Schwartz] alleges was used by a man whom he saw assaulting the woman in Berner Street on the night of the murder, was not addressed to the supposed accomplice but to Schwartz himself. It appears that since the Lipski case it has come to be used as an epithet in addressing or speaking of Jews." [12]

It is unquestionably true that the prejudice directed toward Jews diminished the weight of Schwartz's testimony concerning the two men he witnessed at the murder scene. Apparently the police authorities as well as the members of the inquest jury determined that the two men were not acting in partnership to commit the crime.

Without further investigation, there was no certainty that the two persons witnessed at the murder scene were strangers to each other. Yet there was no further investigation of the pair; prejudice had glossed over the facts.

In book after book on the subject of the Whitechapel murders researchers and writers on criminology have reported incredulously on the ineffectiveness of the London police division. The most proficient and renowned investigators of Scotland Yard were effectively emasculated, it seems, by the antics of a ghoulish murderer.

The ineffectiveness of the police bore little relation to the acclaimed guile of Jack the Ripper; it was far more firmly grounded in the amorphous attitudes and prejudices against the Jews of Whitechapel. As with all mysteries, the surrounding circumstances are usually simple, but elusive. The mystery begins to unravel with the recognition of how anti-Semitic feelings in the community affected police activity.

I bring your attention back to the murder of Elizabeth Stride, when a message was chalked on the wall at Goulston Street. "The Juwes [or Jewes] are not the men that will be blamed for nothing."[13]

It was an attempt to divert attention to the Jews as the group harboring the killer and to inflame the public against the Jews. Recognizing the potential consequences, the police quickly washed away the markings in order to prevent any local uprising against the Jews in that community.

Wide-ranging anti-Semitism, which more than likely reflected the feelings of government officials (from the local constabulary to the royal family) as well as of society in general (and the murderer, no doubt), not only tainted the minds of the investigators but, in conjunction with a shortage of manpower and popular panic, also prevented discovery of the murderer.

My theory is that there had to be two persons in homicidal harmony, who knew each other very well. And it seemed clear

111

from the exhaustive police investigations that neither one resided in the community where the murders occurred. Rather, they came into the Whitechapel area at the close of the week or the weekend, when the murders were committed. Obviously, they lived a short distance from the East End of London. Equally obviously, they were kindred souls.

The identities of the murderers began to unfold before my eyes as one confirmation after another emerged from my research. The mystery of a century had remained unsolved, on one side, due to police bewilderment. But, on the other side, there appeared also to be a cover-up of certain facts and circumstances.

I have consistently asserted, and do so again, that the Whitechapel murders were expressions of a sexually perverted person. Now I was convinced that the crimes had been committed by two persons—perverted partners.

Contemporary gossip had claimed Prince Eddy as the one who committed the murders, but no firm basis was ever established for the accusation. I decided to delve further into the rumors. It had to be more than his noted attendance at homosexual clubs. Homicides are not reserved for any particular type of sexual preference. What piqued my interest was the tutorial relationship and lingering friendship between Prince Eddy and J. K. Stephen. I was convinced that the basis for the rumors circulating around Prince Eddy lay in his interaction with J. K. Stephen. I turned my full attention to Mr. Stephen.

The basic facts about J. K.'s birth and education were readily available. However, my determined search for information concerning his personal experiences or background was consistently thwarted. How else would I discover whether he had the characteristics to be the Whitechapel murderer? If he did, his personality would show signs of sexual perversion and disorder.

I had almost given up when I stumbled upon a study by A. C. Benson published in 1911. It was a series of biographies of men whom Benson, a distinguished writer and academic, had known at

Eton, one of whom was J. K. Stephen. The book provided several leads into J. K.'s lifestyle, but it turned out to be the proverbial tip of the iceberg.[14]

A friend's description of J. K. Stephen during his early years at school was recorded in Benson's book:

> When I entered college at Eton in 1874, Jem Stephen, as he was always called, had been there three years. I do not remember my first actual sight of him, but he was so entirely unlike other boys that, once seen, it was impossible to forget him. He had a very big head with fine, clear-cut features, large and rather terrific eyes, a strong expressive mouth, and a solid chin. He wore his hair, which curled slightly, somewhat long and parted in the middle. The expression of his face was severe to grimness in repose—it was eminently a judicial face—though it lit up with an irrepressible smile. He gave the impression of enormous strength. He was very sturdily built and walked in a slow, ungainly, and almost shuffling manner, holding his hands stiffly at his sides, his fingers extended. He was very much of a hero among the smaller boys for several rather inconsequential reasons.[15]

J. K.'s outward appearance created a strong impression. His "terrific eyes" could conjure up a frightening or terrifying reaction. His body showed signs of rigidity and stiffness while walking, which, to me, indicated a rigid, inflexible personality. A noteworthy point is that he was a hero among the smaller boys, but I differ strongly from the observer who thought the reasons inconsequential. Quite the contrary, the reasons were deeply rooted in his sexual fantasies. As a matter of fact, J. K. was very fond of small boys and played with them, not innocently and not naively. The love for such children expressed his pedophilia. One type of sexual disorder is often an indicator that other perversions are present. I proceeded to find out what they were.

His older brother, Herbert Stephen, reported that "James Kenneth Stephen was born in London on 25 February 1859. He was

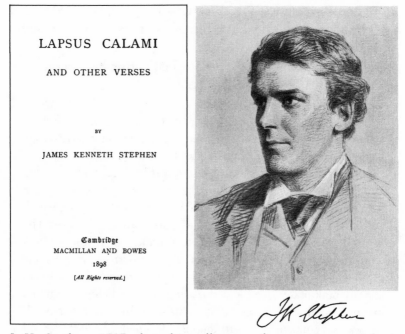

LAPSUS CALAMI

AND OTHER VERSES

BY

JAMES KENNETH STEPHEN

Cambridge
MACMILLAN AND BOWES
1898
[All Rights reserved.]

J. K. Stephen, 1887, from his collection of verses, *Lapsus Calami*. (*Macmillan & Bowes, Cambridge*)

the second son of his famous father Sir James Fitzjames Stephen (1829–1894), who in 1879 became a Criminal Court Judge—Mr. Justice Stephen. In 1868, J. K. Stephen went to a school at Southborough near Tunbridge Wells, kept by the Reverend W. D. Wheeler, and in the following year to the Reverend W. T. Browning's school at Thorpe Mandeville, Banbury, which then had a great reputation as a preparatory school for College at Eton. [The scholars at Eton form a privileged group, or College, within the school.] In 1871, he was elected a colleger at Eton, being placed second on the list, and he remained at Eton until Easter 1878, being the pupil first of Mr. Oscar Browning . . ."[16]

J. K. Stephen's schooling was steeped in religious tenets. One may expect that as an adult his beliefs would reflect such pious training. It was quite the opposite: J. K. emerged with an anticlerical attitude and later became an agnostic. While at school he focused only on the subjects he liked. He became a serious student of history at the expense of learning classics or mathematics. Nevertheless, he did well in school and was eventually awarded an Eton scholarship at King's College, Cambridge, a goal he had set for himself in 1878, when he graduated at nineteen, "the usual age for leaving school."[17]

The Stephen tribe—I use the word deliberately—was dominated by industrious and competitive males. The members, men and women alike, were proud of their affiliation with the family. They were also jealous of each other, as well as of outsiders who tried to emulate them. The seniors in the family, the writer Leslie Stephen and his older brother Judge Fitzjames, were revered and admired. James Fitzjames Stephen's most famous work was a *History of the Criminal Law in England*, published in 1883. He remained a judge until 1891, when he fell afoul of public opinion, which was critical of his conduct of the famous Maybrick murder trial.

Florence Maybrick was convicted on August 7, 1889, of poisoning her husband with arsenic, and condemned to death. Judge Fitzjames Stephen made known his belief in the inherent evil of women. During the trial he told the jury, without presenting any evidence, that Mrs. Maybrick was an adulteress, and that an adulteress by nature was likely to commit murder.[18]

Public outrage against him became so threatening that he had to be given police protection and was forced to resign from the bench. Although he held to his belief that the wife had administered the poison, he finally conceded that it was also possible Mr. Maybrick had died from other causes. In the end, Mrs. Maybrick was reprieved and sentenced to life imprisonment.

One of the judge's strongest defenders was his brother, Leslie Stephen, a renowned philosopher and journalist, best known today as the father of Virginia Woolf.

Let us look more closely into the emotional relationships of the

Stephen family. Thanks to Leslie Stephen's biography of his brother, we know a good deal about them.[19]

The maternal ancestors of James Fitzjames and Leslie Stephen were descendants of the Venn family, who belonged to an Evangelical sect. They traced their lineage back through a long line of clergymen beginning in the reign of Queen Elizabeth. James Fitzjames Stephen considered the Venns to be of higher moral and religious character than the Stephens, and often referred to their resolute nature as a major influence in neutralizing the "irritable and nervous temperament" of many Stephens.

The term "nervous temperament" usually connotes a mild form of restlessness, slight anxiety or a faint depression. It is in the lower range of emotional upset and may go unnoticed, even by the sufferer, who thinks it will pass if he keeps constantly busy. Some of the subtle indications of emotional upset are forgetfulness, lack of concentration, boredom or fatigue. The more serious types of emotional upset may lead to daydreaming, nausea, indigestion, loss of appetite, insomnia (or the converse of excessive need for sleep), hesitancy in speaking, frequent slips of the tongue, depression, hyperactivity, inability to relax, difficulty in coordinating one's ability with one's ambitions, lack of sexual potency, concealment of one's feelings, and secretiveness.

Fitzjames's character was "marked by adversity to any display of feeling." When Fitzjames was only four years old, he told his brother Leslie, "You should keep your love locked up as I do." At the age of six, he was pondering, "How do you know the world is not a dream?"[20]

At another time, according to Leslie Stephen, Fitzjames complained of having "naughty thoughts." Their father, who was considerably older than those of Fitzjames's friends, told him to stop thinking about them—to concentrate on "sending them away." Fitzjames followed this advice and afterward declared that he was so proud of sending the thoughts away that he "wants to keep them so that he may send them away." The "naughty thoughts" were never revealed, but we may safely say that they depicted some form of violence or sex.[21]

This stern home environment was passed down to the judge's own family and had a strong effect upon J. K.'s emotional and sexual development. In one incident, Fitzjames refused to give J. K. any rewards for good behavior because, he reasoned, it would make him "do right from a wrong motive."[22] Such obstructions of the boy's feelings during his childhood produced a devastating personality disorder, sexual in nature, which subsequently enforced the suppression and repression of his feelings.

The subliminal effects of such growing experiences are lodged in the unconscious mind and determine our future conduct. Subliminal effects are extremely difficult to trace, because what appears to be the *cause* of such irregular conduct may be merely the conduit for the stored subliminal feelings. The demanding and selfish nature of Fitzjames produced strong feelings of guilt leading to subsequent mental depression for both father and son.

Visible symptoms of emotional upset surfaced in several members of the Stephen clan, viewed by Quentin Bell and Leonard Woolf—both in a position to know—as notoriously hypersensitive, nervous, irritable, opinionated, rigid, and generally difficult to get along with.[23] They worked hard and persistently for long periods, often displaying the "down" side of their manic tendencies by silence, introversion and, eventually, depression.

In the home where J. K. grew up, intellectual activity was held in the highest esteem. Everyone with whom he came in contact aspired and achieved. He competed with his father for recognition, as well as with the other children. His sense of identity and self-esteem was closely identified with acts of achievement and authority. Everyone was engrossed in his or her own activities, which left little tolerance or time for a crying, clinging, or unruly child. At an early age, he learned to hide his personal reflections and feelings—often behind words with double meanings, which often needed to be clarified or interpreted in order to be understood. We may assume that in the face of constant frustration in getting attention from any member of the family, J. K.'s despair and apprehension would intermittently explode into anger and hate.

Young children, boys and girls alike, often harbor thoughts of violent or sexual encounters. In order to avoid his father's detection of such prohibited ideas, J. K. coined words of dual intent. It was like a personal game of inventing new words, places and names in a code known only to him—and later, perhaps, to his close friend.

J. K. was esteemed by his friends for his ability to write light verse, and he would often toss off impromptu lines they regarded as exceptionally witty. He published two slim volumes of these, entitled *Lapsus Calami* and *Quo Musa Tandis?*, which went through more than one edition and were subsequently republished as *Lapsus Calami and other Verses* by his brother Herbert Stephen in March 1892, after J. K. Stephen's death. Herbert Stephen's introduction and the poems themselves contain much additional information about the poet.[24]

J. K. was also adept at slinging verbal abuse and insults. Benson's book describes his emotional outbursts as ". . . the most copious and prodigious flow of elaborate bad language that ever issued from human lips. It was not obscene language, and he always bore an absolutely stainless character, but it was incredibly direct and supremely opprobrious; and on the rare occasions when he lost his temper, the terror of the situation was much modified by the amazing variety of expression with which he gave the rein to his feelings."[25]

We may reasonably assume that J. K.'s frustration and anger erupted in verbal tirades, rife with insults and curses. His violent outbursts may be described as temper tantrums, and I felt certain that these occurred on more than the "rare occasions" reported by Benson. Such tantrums, however, would not have begun at Eton; they were derived from a fearful childhood, as is usually the case. As he grew into boyhood, he experienced additional periods of emotional upset concerning his mother, on top of already accumulated fears and frustrations. Such repetition compounded the sensations of fear, insecurity and being cut off, or castration.

It is clear from Benson's account that J. K. was cursing and using abusive language as a young adult of perhaps seventeen or eighteen. Having temper tantrums at that stage of life is a fairly accurate gauge of a disturbed personality. His language exhibited signs of the jealousy, fear and rejection he had experienced during his childhood and youth and demonstrated his continuing efforts to hold off his anxiety about being left alone.

Tantrums are a mode of venting disappointments, but they are also calls for help. A flaring temper indicates simultaneously a desire for attention and a cry of despair. We have all seen a child throw himself on the floor with arms flailing and legs kicking at the air. Sometimes children "grow out of it," leaving little emotional residue. More often, they are left starved for attention and with feelings of anger and rejection, aimed largely at the mother.

I found it particularly interesting that there was virtually no mention of J. K. Stephen's mother in any of the sources I uncovered, which reported only on the male members of the family. We do know her name—Mary Richenda Cunningham, the daughter of a clergyman. She married James Fitzjames Stephen in 1855 and outlived both her husband and her second son. In 1892, as J. K. lay near death in St. Andrew's Hospital, Northampton, England, he refused to read three letters his mother had written to him. Lady Stephen visited him there and was at his bedside when he died a few days later. [26]

J. K.'s early severance from his mother instigated his hostile feelings toward women. As far as J. K. was concerned, his mother had no emotional significance and, therefore, he didn't feel any need to have a relationship with her. To calm his fears and threats of emotional upset, he stayed aloof from her, denigrating her as a human being. He was afraid of her, and what you fear, you hate. [27]

His mother made him feel weak and ineffectual. Signs of his

sexual repression began to surface when he turned his preference toward young boys. Emasculated by the rejection of his mother, he sought refuge in more amenable partners.

It was his idea "that age and standing in the school should be no bar to friendship and so [he and his friends] deliberately made friends with several small boys who seemed to be interested in the same things. Of course, the proceeding was not approved by the Sixth Form set [seniors]; and they were not wholly justified in their disapproval."[28]

We must assume from this slightly naive account, I think, that J. K. had already discovered his longing for boys, and that the rationale for making friends with the younger boys was sexual in nature. Using his intelligence, he created an environment to foster such friendships and the pleasures derived from them.

Having been indoctrinated with his father's perception of women as evil, J. K. recoiled from his mother and viewed her as overbearing and dangerous. In order to overcome his fear of her, he fantasized her as well as himself as devoid of human qualities. When frustration culminated in violent outbursts, J. K. felt no human emotion.

J. K.'s fondness for young children was a gender disorder. Feeling castrated in his familial relationships, he had difficulty in establishing his masculine identity. Perversion is an expression of castration and J. K. continually participated in perverse activities.

Benson described J. K. as a man with a penchant for inventing sobriquets and assumed names. The clever pseudonym of "Jack the Ripper" was clearly reflective of the women ripped to pieces. It is natural to conclude that Stephen was the man who signed the name "Jack the Ripper" on the famous postcard sent to the Central News Agency in London. Surprisingly, the police and press never mentioned the name "Jack the Ripper" until after the double murders of Stride and Eddowes had been carried out on the night of September 30, 1888. The card had been received by the editor on September 27, two days earlier, and forwarded to Scotland

120

Yard, where the inspectors, in the early stages of the Ripper investigations, thought the message was a hoax.

The Whitechapel murders had to be committed by a person or persons of considerable physical strength. Participation in sports provides muscular development as well as an acceptable outlet for violent fantasies, but when I began my research I could find no mention of J. K.'s having engaged in any such activities. It was a missing link in my concept of his personality and my belief in his propensity for physical violence.

I found the missing link in Benson's book, which gave an account of how Stephen "played the odd game of football known as the Wall Game with remarkable skill and endurance." The Wall Game is a form of football unique to Eton, in which one side defends a famous wall, instead of a goal, while the other endeavors to reach and scale it. It is said to be chiefly an excuse for a series of scrimmages of massive proportions with few holds barred, from which participants emerge covered with mud.[29]

Herbert Stephen also described his brother's athletic activities:

> His fortune here was not dissimilar to the fortune he had obtained in his school work. Being big, heavy, and very strong, he took naturally to the "Wall game" of football, in which I think from the first, he always occupied the position of "Wall," and for summer diversion became a "wet-bob." [Eton's term for a member of one of the school's rowing crews.]
>
> He got his "College Wall" colours, if I remember right, in 1874, and was Captain or "Keeper of the Wall" in 1876 or 1877 . . . I believe he was one of the best "Walls" who ever played the game, and for at least ten years—that is, nearly the rest of his life—he took a great interest in it, and seldom failed to take an eleven to play the College team of the year.[30]

J. K.'s continuing and overwhelming interest in the Eton Wall Game was fueled by a compelling desire to win and express his manliness. He was plagued by his urge to act out his violent impulses, resorting to either manic work or manic conduct. Eventually, he would be unable to control such impulses or to channel them into acceptable forms of behavior.

In 1878, at the age of nineteen, J. K. Stephen came into residence at King's College, Cambridge, and soon became one of the better known undergraduates of his time. He won many university honors, among them the Member's Prize for an English essay, the Whewell Scholarship for International Law, and the Winchester Reading Prize. At the beginning of his career at Cambridge, he wrote letters to a younger friend, who described them as follows:

> They [the letters] were extravagantly absurd and fantastic, never about anything in particular. They would be very cryptic to the ordinary reader because of their allusions and nicknames.[31]

As I see it, J. K. consistently demonstrated a desperate need for secrecy and for the sardonic expression of his "forbidden" feelings. The more he suppressed his thoughts, however, the more they preoccupied him. Thereafter, the proverbial snowball effect took over. The more he was preoccupied, the more he became depressed. The more he was depressed, the more he sought pleasure and distraction. And so on down the road of mental instability and confusion.

It is important to note that J. K.'s search for pleasure was not directed toward women, but toward men. At one point, just before his fatal illness, he made violent advances toward Stella Duckworth, who was the daughter of his aunt, Julia Stephen, Leslie's second wife, by her first marriage. But there is no indication of any other adult relationship with a woman. Even his attempts with Stella, recounted more fully in Chapter Eight, were a desperate side trip to demonstrate his masculinity. In fact, he hated women; the extent of his condemnation surfaced later in his published works.

The combination of his covert personality and preference for men led J. K. naturally to a secret society called the Apostles. Founded in 1820 as a debating group by twelve Christian scholars, its original purposes included offering its members an opportunity to discuss, privately, the difficulties and doubts they had about their Christian philosophy. The society earned a reputation as a semi-secret, semi-mystical organization. As it became more sinister, it also became more elite. At the time J. K. was a member, the organization was centered in Trinity College and the homosexual undertones of the group had gained momentum and influence. According to the Apostles' maxim, "the love of man for man is greater than that of man for woman, a philosophy known to the Apostles as the higher sodomy."[32]

Howells and Skinner noted that "the Apostles formed a secret society who, very much helped by their homosexual orientation, were able to find appointment within the establishment. It is stated that selection was made without sexual predilections. *This is unadulterated nonsense.* [author's emphasis] . . . In the 1930s this same group, with the same undercurrent of homosexuality, engendered the most notorious spy ring in modern times."[33]

The Apostles society afforded a perfect outlet for J. K. Stephen, providing camaraderie as well as a sense of power to indulge in his "forbidden" feelings. He adapted easily to its secrecy and found within it confirmation of his own homosexual tendencies and misogynistic feelings. He formed a close friendship with Harry F. Wilson from the group, who was later included in the close circle of friends around Prince Eddy.

Not surprisingly, no incidents of homosexual activity by any members of the Apostles are on record. But the absence of such reports does not reflect the absence of homosexual interaction. Secrecy is a rare and coveted virtue, and in those days both secrecy and privacy were honored by strict observance. In addition, at that historical juncture, the discovery of homosexual practices carried appalling penalties of dishonor and imprisonment—as Oscar Wilde found out to his detriment.

J. K. was young, attractive, esteemed as the son of one of Her Majesty's judges and acknowledged for his intelligence and genteel demeanor. He was, to all intents and purposes, the perfect gentleman. If he had acknowledged his homosexual propensities, he would have endangered his social position. His inclinations were safely expressed in light verse, for which he gained acclaim as a poet. His repressions, however, continued to build momentum, which was accompanied by mounting antagonism and egocentricity. Any emotional connection and empathy for others would rapidly have been displaced by concern for his personal interests.

In 1881, Stephen was placed in the first class in the History Tripos, "a success which was particularly satisfactory because no candidate had been placed in the first class in either of the two preceding years . . . At the Union he was elected President in the first [October] term of his third year, an office usually held by the most successful speakers. He was elected a Fellow of King's College in 1885."[34]

J. K.'s striking looks and intellectual brilliance fascinated everyone, young and old. The respected author Dr. James Edmund Vincent arranged to meet him on a visit to Cambridge and was much impressed by his charm and intelligence. That encounter was to lead to the selection of J. K. to serve as tutor for Prince Eddy, who was about to enter the university—and it would become the seed of a new and notorious relationship.

1. Thomas E. Stowell, M.D., "Jack the Ripper: A Solution," *The Criminologist*, November, 1970, p. 40.
2. Michael Harrison, *Clarence, The Life of H.R.H. the Duke of Clarence and Avondale*, 1864–1892, W.H. Allen, London, 1972.
3. Donald Rumbelow, *The Complete Jack the Ripper*, W. H. Allen, London, 1987.
4. Martin Howells and Keith Skinner, *The Ripper Legacy: The Life and*

Death of Jack the Ripper, Sidgwick & Jackson, London, 1987, pp. 175–176.

5. *Ibid.*, p. 158.
6. *Ibid.*, p. 159.
7. *Ibid.*
8. Terence Sharkey, *100 Years of Investigation: The Facts, The Fiction, The Solution*, Ward Lock Ltd., London, 1987, p. 94.
9. Report by Donald S. Swanson, Chief Inspector, *Murder of Elizabeth Stride*, Metropolitan Police, October 19, 1888.
10. Report by Inspector Abberline, *Whitechapel Murders*, Metropolitan Police, November 1, 1888.
11. Memorandum from Office of Home Secretary, Doc. 200–201, November 7, 1888.
12. Letter by Chanin, Office of Home Secretary, November 6, 1888.
13. Stephen Knight, "Jack the Ripper: The Final Solution," *The Criminologist*, November, 1976.
14. Arthur Christopher Benson, *The Leaves of the Tree: Studies in Biography*, G. P. Putnam's Sons, New York/London, 1911.
15. *Ibid.*, pp. 106–107.
16. Herbert Stephen, *Complete and Final Edition of all J. K. Stephen's Poems*, Introduction pp. v–xiii, Putnam & Sons, London, 1893.
17. *Ibid.*
18. Louise De Salvo, *Virginia Woolf: The Impact of Childhood Sexual Abuse on Her Life*, Beacon Press, Boston, 1989, p. 46.
19. Leslie Stephen, *The Life of James Fitzjames Stephen*, London, 1895, p. 69.
20. *Ibid.*
21. *Ibid.*
22. *Ibid.*
23. Quentin Bell, *Virginia Woolf: A Biography*, Harcourt Brace Jovanovich, New York, 1972, p. 35.
24. Herbert Stephen, *op. cit.*
25. Arthur Benson, *op. cit.*, p. 107.
26. Records of St. Andrew's Hospital, Northampton, England, February 4, 1892.
27. David Abrahamsen, M.D., *The Road to Emotional Maturity*, Pren-

tice Hall, New York, 1958, and *The Emotional Care of Your Child*, Simon & Schuster, New York, 1974.

28. Arthur Benson, *op. cit.*, p. 110.
29. *Ibid.*, p. 107.
30. Herbert Stephen, *op. cit.*, pp. v–vi.
31. Arthur Benson, *op. cit.*, p. 34.
32. Martin Howells and Keith Skinner, *op. cit.*, pp. 162–163.
33. *Ibid.*, p. 166.
34. Herbert Stephen, *op. cit.*, pp. vii–viii.

CHAPTER SEVEN

Shadows Over Britain

"What is past is prologue."

SHAKESPEARE,
The Tempest, II, i

WHAT LAY BEHIND the selection of James Kenneth Stephen as tutor for Prince Eddy, the oldest son of the Prince and Princess of Wales? There were other intelligent, charming and learned young men from Eton and Cambridge who were as qualified as he. Besides the seemingly chance encounter with James Vincent, what other reasons could there have been for the young commoner to become the guide and teacher for the heir to the British throne?

According to H. F. Wilson, J. K.'s close friend, Stephen "by general consent was the ablest of the younger generation . . . No better choice could have been made to be Eddy's tutor, for Mr. Stephen, to an extraordinarily brilliant and subtle intellect, united a geniality of disposition that made him, to those who knew him well, one of the most lovable of men. A hearty man was this, and a vigorous, warmhearted, large in mind, versatile in taste, intensely human."[1]

This perceived geniality and warmheartedness were no doubt considerable additional qualifications for the position. Prince Eddy was a shy, backward young man, who, under current standards, may have been characterized as a prime candidate for special attention and education. No doubt his parents felt that this friendly, able young Cambridge don would be the ideal person to nurture whatever latent talents the prince possessed. And this was true—though not in the sense the royal family had intended.

Prince Eddy's low intellectual standard was a persistent source of concern and anxiety for his immediate family and the Queen. Early in his school years, he was described as a dawdler, consistently late, and less able than his younger brother George. His characterization as a slow learner did not change, despite the able tutelage of the Reverend John Neil Dalton during the prince's training as a cadet. Dalton adhered to his teaching task for more than ten years, but in a report to the Prince of Wales, he concluded that "while George [Eddy's brother] has passed all of his subjects as Cadet on *Britannia* [the naval training ship to which both boys were assigned], Eddy failed in all subjects."[2]

According to James Edmund Vincent, who knew the Prince and Princess of Wales well, and who wrote the only authorized biography of the prince, published in 1893:

> The essential things which conduced to the making of his character were the home-life at Sandringham, the life in the woods and on to the stables and on horseback, the period of tutelage at Sandringham when he was being prepared for Cambridge, the life at Cambridge, the tour in India, the life as a cavalry officer, and the brief period of laborious ceremony which he passed as an illustrious personage in an age when princes of the blood work at least as hard as common labourers.[3]

Looking deeper into the prince's home environment at Sandringham in order to uncover the reasons for his failure to develop intellectually and emotionally, I soon found that much of Prince Eddy's life was shrouded in darkness. There has been no detailed study of the psychological and sociological development of Prince

Sir William Withney Gull,
1816–1890. Physician to the
Royal Family. (*Courtesy of*
The New York Academy of
Medicine)

Albert Victor, although Michael Harrison's full-scale biography of
the prince does furnish many details of his personality and lifestyle.

My own research into his life began to unfold in the Library of
the Wellcome Institute for the History of Medicine, London,
where I had come to locate the medical files of the royal physician,
Sir William Withney Gull. I had earlier established from my
research in the archives of the New York Academy of Medicine
that Gull was a distinguished and able physician, well-versed in
the practice of medicine and ahead of his time in the study of
human behavior. He had been in charge of the lunatic wards at
Guy's Hospital in London, and was instrumental in abandoning
the shocking practice of keeping mental patients in chains. Although at one point his name had joined the roster of suspects in
the Whitechapel murders, I could not accept the notion that a
man of such humanity had been involved in such inhuman acts.
But might he have been protecting someone else?

Sir William Gull kept unusually extensive medical reports on his patients, a fact I had confirmed in studying one of his case records. Yet my search in the Wellcome archives, which are part of what is probably the world's most prestigious medical library, turned up only sketchy files of the doctor's work as royal physician. Instead of medical reports, the files contained mainly letters and telegrams between Queen Victoria and the doctor from the year of his appointment in 1872 to 1890. Scattered among the material was a variety of other correspondence to his family and colleagues.

MS 5873. Sir William Withey Gull (1816–1890)
Correspondence and papers, 1863–90, mainly relating to his treatment of the Prince of Wales for typhoid, at Sandringham, 1871–72. Purchased at Sotheby's 16–18 February 1931, lot 406. (acc. 56312).

Summary List.
A/1-97. Medical bulletins on the Prince of Wales.

Drafts, copies and originals, many signed by the Prince's physicians Sir William Jenner, William Gull, and John Lowe, and by his surgeon, Sir James Paget. 25 November 1871–14 January 1872.
B/1-67. Clinical notes on the Prince of Wales. 13 November 1871–15 February 1872, and n.d.
C/1-53. Notes on the Prince of Wales' diet. 26 November 1871–13 January 1872.
D/1-8. Letters to Gull from Queen Victoria. 1872–77
E/1-54. Telegrams to Gull from Queen Victoria. 1871–77 and n.d.
F/1-20. Letters to Gull from various correspondents. 1863–82 and n.d.
G/1-13. Telegrams to Gull from various correspondents. 1871–72.
H/1-9. Drafts and copies of letters and telegrams sent by Gull. 1872–86 and n.d.
I/1-58. Letters from Gull to his son William Cameron Gull (1860–1922), afterwards 2nd Bt. 1869–84 and n.d.
J/1-6. Miscellanea.

From other sources I knew that Dr. Gull had treated Prince Eddy for typhoid fever, and brought him back to health. He had also treated Eddy's father, the Prince of Wales, a few years earlier, for the same illness. There were daily jottings about this case in the file, in keeping with Gull's usual careful itemization of the medical information. Other than this, there were no clinical notes on his royal patients.

Nowhere could I find one word about Prince Eddy's illnesses, or, for that matter, anything else concerning the prince. It had never occurred to me that a physician of such eminence would participate in a medical cover-up. But since there was no mention anywhere of Prince Eddy, whom I knew Gull had also attended, I made the reasonable deduction that certain material had been deliberately removed from the files.

Another dearth of materials I faced was on Eddy's childhood. That was a serious drawback. It is difficult, if not impossible, to understand anyone's personality and behavior without knowledge of his development and experiences as a child. Fortunately, careful analysis of Eddy's family, the roles of his mother and father and their style of bringing up their children, helped me to decipher the young prince's feelings, reactions and character traits during his formative years.

The unique nature of each person depends to a large extent upon his unconscious, which, in turn, reflects his character and influences his conduct. Although specific instances and events encountered in childhood offer the most direct route toward exposing the psyche, it is also possible to determine reliably that person's feelings and ideas, experiences and frustrations, hopes and desires from supplementary reports and records.

J. K. Stephen, for example, relayed in his writings what his feelings and opinions were about women, politics and men. But Prince Eddy never expressed his opinions or feelings—at least not in any public record. The only items found regarding the prince were a few personal letters he had written to his friends, each quite

1876	Morning	Afternoon	Evening	1876	Morning	Afternoon	Even 2
November 24th ?5th Day	104 2/5 P.120		104 3/5 P.120	Dec 14th ?25th	96 3/5 T.96 R.24	T. unable to get it, scraping restless P.88 R.24	T 98 P.88 R 20
" 25th	103 1/5 P.108	1	104 3/5 P.108	" 15th	98. 84.		T 98 P.80 R 20
" 26th	103 1/5 P.108	105 P.132 Dr Hobson	103 P.120 Sir W.Jenner	" 16th	98 84 20		T 99 7/5 P.80 R 20
" 27th ?8th day	103 3/5 P.120	104 3/5 P.120	104 3/5 P.120	" 17th	98 80		T 97 3/5 P.76 R 16
" 28th	103 3/5 P.120 (1.30 AM)103 3/8	105 P.120 103 3/5	104 (6 P.M) P.120 104	" 18th	98 78		T 76
" 29th	104	Sir W Jenner	P.120	" 19.	98. 84		
" 30th	103 3/5 P.120	103 3/5 P.130	7.P.M. 103 11.P.M. 103 3/5				
Dec: 1st ?12th day	103 3/5 P.124	104 3/5 P.132	103 3/5 P.128				
" 2nd	103 P.128 Sir W.Jenner	104 3/5 4 P.M	103 3/5 (2 A.M 103 1/5)				
" 3rd	103 P.120	103 3/5	103 1/5 P.120 Sir W.Gull				
" 4th	102 1/5 P.120	102 4/5 3 P.M P.120	102 3/5 (7 P.M) 103 (11 P.M) P.120				
" 5th	103 P.118	102 4/5 (4 P.M) Res. 42	103 (11 P.M) P.118 R.40				
" 6th	104 P.120 R.40	103 1/5 (3.30) P.120 R.40	103 3/5 P.120 R.38				
" 7th ?18th day	103 1/5 P.120 R.38	103 P.112 R.38	103 1/5 P.112 R.34				
" 8th	101 3/5 P.118 R.36	101 3/5 P.120 R.36 Sir W Gull	102 P.120 R.34				
" 9th	103 P.124 R.36	102 3/5 P.124 R.34	102 3/5 P.120 R 36				
" 10th ?21st day	101 3/5 P.120 R.36	101 P.120 P.36	(6 P.M)102 R.32 (11 P.M)100				
" 11th	98 3/5 P.105 R.31	97 1/5 P.89 R.26 Sir W.Gull	P.110 R.31 96 P.98 R.25				
" 12th	97 P.100 R.30	98 3/5 3 P.M P.112 R.35	99 7 P.M P.110 R.32 11 P.M R.28				
" 13th	97 3/5 P.98 R.26	97 P.92 R.25	97 3/5 P.89 R.24				

All these temperatures were taken with the same thermometer

Morning generally at 10.a.m
Afternoon at 3.p.m
& Evening generally at 10.p.m except where mentioned as some other time.

M.S 5873
J/2

56312

Temperature
Prince of Wales at Sandringham
Dec 1876

A detailed case history from 1876 in Dr. Gull's own handwriting.
(*Courtesy of The Wellcome Institute for the History of Medicine, London*)

pleasant and polite and totally lacking in any social or political statement. The few short speeches that he made were obviously written for him, again indicating his inability to communicate. The prince, it appeared, was a *tabula rasa*—an empty mind. But even at a clean table there are always a few crumbs on the plate.

Prince Albert Victor Christian Edward of Wales was born at Frogmore House, Windsor, on January 8, 1864. He was the first child of Edward, Prince of Wales and his wife Princess Alexandra and consequently heir to the throne, after his father. The baby was born unexpectedly, two months before full term, and weighed only three and three-quarter pounds.

I was shocked and surprised to discover that no preparations had been made for the birth of the infant. The weather was exceptionally cold and bitter and there were not even appropriate blankets and baby clothes available. No nurse, no doctor, no midwife was present. In fact, the history books are unclear on where the Prince of Wales was at the time of the birth. A government official, however, *was* present, adhering to a rule originating centuries earlier, in order to certify that the child was a legitimate member of the royal family.

A short time after Prince Eddy's precipitate entrance into the world, his parents found a woman to take care of the newborn baby. From the outset, his life was cloaked in rejection and mystery.

Eddy's mother was the Danish Princess Alexandra Caroline. She was born in 1844 and was married on March 10, 1863, to Prince Albert Edward ("Bertie"), Queen Victoria's second child and eldest son. Resentment toward her mother-in-law arose early in her marriage, when Germany violently attacked and invaded her Danish homeland while Queen Victoria, who sympathized strongly with the Germans, made no objection. Later, and throughout Alexandra's marriage, the Queen persistently intervened in the rearing of Alexandra's children. The Queen asserted that she "has the right to speak out about the raising of the children, because she was of the Windsor family."[4]

Queen Victoria poses wistfully with the stone surrogate of her Prince
Consort after the marriage of the Prince and Princess of Wales, 1863.

The Princess of Wales by Richard Lauchert, 1863.

All of this contributed to the Princess's feelings of alienation from the rest of the royal family. Moreover, Alexandra lived with another disturbing condition. Queen Victoria, having been widowed by the early death of Prince Albert in 1861, had become pathologically obsessed by her much-beloved husband. For example, she kept his chamber as if he were still alive, with his nightshirt laid out every night, and the chamber pot cleaned with hot water every morning. The Queen supervised these rituals carefully. Princess Alexandra became a silent witness to the grim spectacle.

In 1865, Alexandra gave birth to a second son, who was destined to become King George V. He, too, was born prematurely—one month early. Over the next four years, she gave birth to three girls, born in 1867, 1868 and 1869. One of her daughters, Maud, became the Queen of Norway. Alexander, the youngest and last child, was born in 1871 but survived for only a few hours. Whether he was premature is not known. Of the six children born to the Princess of Wales, two arrived prematurely and one died within a few hours of birth.

The Prince of Wales was consistently absent from home. Given his constant search for pleasures and amusements, it is difficult to imagine that Bertie could develop a genuine love toward a woman. Even as a young adolescent having hardly gone through puberty, he sought the company of young girls, and this precociousness upset the Consort and Queen Victoria. The best solution they could think of was to find someone to marry him. I believe he may have been coerced into the marriage and that grave consequences for Alexandra and their children, perhaps in particular Prince Eddy who was the oldest of them, were the result.

Already in 1877, when Eddy was thirteen years old, he undoubtedly began to hear about his father's escapades with Lillie Langtry, his mistress.[5] Although the family and the English press tried to keep it a secret, it was acknowledged in Court circles. He was simply out to enjoy himself and take his pleasures where he

Sandringham House.

could find them. It appeared that he was totally preoccupied with women. They presented to him a mystique that he wanted to possess, regardless of personal and family cost.

Although Bertie took some interest in his son off and on, he most certainly did not serve as a healthy and helpful role model for his sons or daughters, particularly for Eddy. Alexandra tried to take her husband's failings in her stride, but her marital situation was too complex. Her husband's infidelity, coupled with the Queen's constant interference and peculiar involvement with her deceased husband, helped to increase the turmoil and unhappiness suffered by Princess Alexandra. Those same emotional factors were present in the life of her eldest son.

The general theory is that children who are born prematurely

The Wales family, circa 1888. From the left, standing: Prince George, the Princess of Wales, the Prince of Wales, Princess Victoria. Seated: Princess Maud, Prince Albert Victor (Eddy), Princess Louise.

At Marlborough House, 1889. Standing, left to right: Duke of Clarence (Eddy), Princess Maud (later Queen of Norway), the Princess of Wales, Princess Louise (later Duchess of Fife), the Prince of Wales. Sitting: Prince George, Princess Victoria.

develop more slowly—physically, emotionally and intellectually. Although George, his younger brother, was also premature, Eddy was by far the more passive and fearful of the two.

Eddy was described as backward, a slow learner, dull-witted and absent-minded. He was often seen daydreaming, and was sometimes perceived as mentally defective, unable to grasp simple concepts. Alexandra was concerned and upset when the boys' tutor Dalton recommended that Eddy should be removed from the Navy training vessel *Britannia*, his standard of intelligence "being too low to make it possible for him to compete with the average cadet."[6]

She did not accept the recommendation. She wrote back that

Eddy must remain on the *Britannia* with his younger brother George. Her decision was based partly on Eddy's dependency on his younger brother and partly on a misguided attempt to save Eddy from being embarrassed and humiliated because of his limited mental capacity. It was a foolhardy decision, one of the first of many attempts to cover up Eddy's brain dysfunction.

Future cover-ups became routine, without family dispute or disturbance. The objective was to protect Eddy, and the objective was accomplished—to an extent far beyond what was contemplated.

Another theory explaining Eddy's difficulties attributed his backwardness to a possible hearing defect, thought to be inherited from his mother, who became completely deaf at the age of twenty-six. Alexandra's hearing defect was caused by otosclerosis, a fusing of the three small bones in the inner ear, a condition she inherited from her mother. The disease may lie dormant until precipitated, for instance, by pregnancy.

Whether or not Eddy's learning disability was connected with a hearing defect, there is no indication that the family sought professional help. One reason may be that Alexandra resisted it in order not to expose her own deafness. But the Princess's care and concern for her children were well-known, and it is likely that she would have talked with one of the royal physicians about this possible defect in her oldest son. Strange as it may sound, Alexandra may not have realized that her son was deaf, because of her own deafness. A great deal of information about Eddy's health was also deliberately withheld from her and others by the royal physicians, so as not to interfere with his eventual ascension to the throne.

His backwardness and absentmindedness, coupled with the fact that his mind seemed to be shut off from his environment, made me ponder whether his mental shortcomings were induced by mild symptoms of epilepsy.

I also took into account that no one in the family read a book, strange as that may seem. Surely, reading and writing would be a requisite for anyone who would be called upon to become the King. Dalton, after years of teaching him, came to the conclusion that Eddy was beyond any learning; Dalton was thoroughly disgusted with his princely pupil. I have treated children who, despite vigorous support from the teacher, were unable to grasp the written or spoken word. They have a learning disability—a reading and a writing disability. For such children, written words are hard to understand because the letters jump around the page. They suffer from dyslexia, and so did Prince Eddy.

Such a disability explains Eddy's backwardness. His inability to participate in sophisticated conversation, or to give an apt answer, was a reflection of his educational handicap. Despite the many efforts he made, he could not comprehend fully the written word. A dyslexic person is prone to feelings of helplessness and confusion.

At the time when Eddy was learning to read and write, nobody knew about dyslexia. Dyslexia, as we now know, is an inherited condition that can be passed from one generation to the next. There was no information about any dyslexia in the royal family, but that fact, in itself, did not mean much since the condition had not been previously defined.

In my native country of Norway, there were some unofficial whisperings that King Olav had difficulty in reading and writing. King Olav was the son of Princess Maud, sister of Prince Eddy. In 1906, she became Queen of Norway. Princess Astrid, a daughter of King Olav, admitted on public television on September 18, 1990 that she and her family had difficulties in learning to read and write.

She said, "I complained all the time that I didn't see. The others perceived it as quite something different of what had been written on the blackboard than I did."[7]

Dyslexia was one basic reason for Prince Eddy's lack of understanding of reading and writing and his lack of participation in the emotional and social life expected from a son destined to be a king.

141

His mother Alexandra's early experiences offer some other insights into Eddy's emotional and intellectual underdevelopment. She was an exceptionally beautiful woman, who could easily identify with the fairy princess in Hans Christian Andersen's stories. As a young girl she was somewhat of a tomboy, with a quick temper and a deplorable habit of tardiness, which was to mark her throughout her long life. She also displayed an affectionate and passionate nature.

In a fairytale existence, all wishes are fulfilled. She may have expected a happy ending for her marriage and her children. She may have naively believed that childbirth just "happened" and that she and the child would always be taken care of. Perhaps the arrival of Eddy, her firstborn, was the rude harbinger of discomfort and unhappiness in her marital union.

His mother's emotional gyrations militated against Eddy's chances of a normal childhood. As a baby, apparently, he was not welcomed by her. Was she afraid of giving birth? Did she not realize that she was pregnant? Was her rejection based upon her dislike of her husband's womanizing? Eventually, of course, the Prince of Wales left her behind as he expanded his bachelor-like social activities—partygoing, hunting, traveling and cavorting with beautiful women.

Loneliness would drive Alexandra closer to her children. The older boys, Eddy and George, became extraordinarily attached to her and she to them. Whether consciously or unconsciously, she retarded their emotional and intellectual development in order to prolong their childlike dependency. Her correspondence with them during their adolescence and early adulthood reveals her own ingenuous and immature disposition. In what have been characterized as "MotherDear letters," she asked them to think of her as the most important person in their lives. One letter to George, when he was in his twenties and a naval officer, closes as if directed to a small child, "With a great big kiss for your lovely little face."[8]

The correspondence between her sons also reflected their close involvement with their mother. Eddy wrote to his brother George, "If MotherDear has thought of the communion for us on Sunday, that is the only thing that could bring me back to Sandringham before Tuesday."[9]

Princess Alexandra was more involved with being a mother to her sons than with her status as the Princess of Wales and potential Queen Consort. In strong contrast was Queen Victoria, whose regal attitude continually reminded everyone that she was the Queen.

One can commiserate with Princess Alexandra for keeping the two older children tied to her. She surely did not intend to retard their development. But the result was stagnation for both as immature adolescents, far behind their chronological progression.

Eddy, in particular, was much like Peter Pan—passive, frightened and cloaking his dependency with impulsive bravado. He had little, if any, sophistication and often appeared lost—which made him an easy prey for stronger wills to exploit.

"MotherDear" was a Wendy type, who encouraged her offspring to remain with her in innocence and fantasy. Eddy could be the handsome young prince, she the beautiful princess. It was an opportunity to revive the fairytale existence she remembered from her Danish childhood.

The relationship between Eddy and his parents was filled with deep-seated conflicts. On one side was his devoted, egocentric, mild-mannered but dominating mother. On the other was his father—critical, competitive and frequently hostile. His nickname for his older son—who habitually wore high, starched collars and gleaming cuffs in an effort to hide his unnaturally long thin neck and wrists—was "Collars and Cuffs," which amply expresses his sardonic, critical and unloving attitude. No doubt the Prince of Wales was influenced by the sense of disapproval with which his own parents had surrounded him throughout his life; it is those who have suffered abuse as children who most frequently become abusers in their turn.

Whatever the cause, the intensity of his father's demands on him must have compounded Eddy's sense of helplessness and desperation, driving him further into the trap of maternal obsession. Such closeness to his mother was bound to result in hatred of anyone who competed with his emotional claims on her. It was the classic oedipal relationship experienced by many young boys. But, unlike most of these, Eddy's emotional attachment to his mother lasted throughout his life and was only finally terminated by his death at the age of twenty-eight.

Like his mother, Eddy wanted to remain a child, yearned to be taken care of, and preferred to be free of responsibility. These thoughts and inclinations surfaced after he and George parted to pursue separate higher education. Eddy wrote his brother: "My dear George. So we are at last separated for the first time and I can't tell you how strange it seems to be without you and how much I miss everything all day long."[10]

In Vincent's biography of Eddy, he states that "when Eddy in his babyhood came to change his diet, he showed the strongest possible aversion to animal food."[11] There are two points to be made there, that Eddy did not want any changes in his daily life, wishing like a child to hold on to what had always been the routine, and that as a child he disliked animal food. It quite often happens that children protest against changing from milk to solid food, but that a child at such a tender age should show a marked animosity may have some psychological importance, especially in view of his later pronounced interest in shooting and killing animals. Was this desire to hunt a carryover from his hatred of animal food as a child? And did this hate also involve human beings?

It is possible that he was afraid of animals. Feeling threatened by them, he had to get rid of them by every means available. His obsession, as a young man, with shooting birds, animals, whatever was in front of him, enabled him to show his power.

A telling incident took place when Eddy was still a youngster, possibly twelve years old. According to the Grand Duchess Xenia

144

of Russia, Eddy's cousin, "while boating on Lake Fredensborg with the family one day, Eddy suddenly picked up his sisters' little dog and threw it into the water. 'Why did you do that?' asked his astonished grandfather [possibly Czar Alexander II, but more probably King Christian IX of Denmark], pushing him in over the side. Eddy seemed quite unconcerned as he scrambled back into the boat, announcing rather unnecessarily that he was very wet. 'Of course you're very wet,' snapped his grandfather, 'you've been in the lake.' 'Why did you do that to me?' 'Because you did it to the little dog.' "[12] John Van Der Kiste commented: "Such feeble-mindedness is not altogether without its more comic side, but the idea of a King of England who, as Xenia said, never *minded* [italics in original] anything, was not something to contemplate with equanimity."[13]

Eddy did not care or did not understand that the consequence of his throwing the animal into the water would be that the dog would be drowned. Instead, he complained about being wet and could not comprehend why his grandfather had pushed him in after the dog. Throwing the dog over the side might seem like an act of impulse. But was it really that impulsive? The act might well have expressed hatred and utter contempt for the animal, in contrast to the prince's concern for his own life. Might he already as a child have had murder in his mind?

Like Peter Pan, Eddy remained a child emotionally, intellectually and sexually. His attempts to simulate adulthood could not camouflage his boyish tendencies. Even his hormones would not cooperate, creating only enough facial hair to grow a small moustache, which he waxed and turned up at the ends as an expression of his masculinity.

To further compensate for a lack of manly demeanor, Eddy became a great hunter and practiced the sport skillfully during his jaunts to Scotland. His marksmanship brought down all kinds of animals and birds. In concert with other members of the aristocracy, he had become a professional killer.

Prince Albert Victor Edward in
the Uniform of the Tenth Hussars.
(*Sketch by W. E. Hays*)

To complete the image of manhood, he favored wearing a uniform. Members of the royal family frequently wore uniforms, as if to emphasize their importance and authority. Pictures of Eddy in the uniform of a lieutenant-colonel of the Tenth Hussars at Aldershot in 1891 depict a man seemingly content with military life. In fact, according to Michael Harrison, Eddy viewed his military life as a bore, although his liking for the uniform kept him loyal to the commitment. But how good a soldier could he have been when, as Harrison tells us, he had forgotten six times to put on his soldier's belt?

Prince Eddy dining at Hall, Trinity College, circa 1884.

The Prince and Princess of Wales were well aware of their son's mental difficulties. For Eddy to take up his position as the future King, immediate action was required to stir him from his intellectual and emotional lethargy. The security of the British throne was at stake.

With the same determination the Princess had shown in keeping her two sons together, she embarked on finding a young tutor who could also serve as a companion to the heir. Since Eddy would enter Trinity College, Cambridge, in 1883, the matter was of importance.

J. K. Stephen was interviewed at Sandringham and retained to prepare Eddy for Cambridge, and subsequently to guide him through his studies at Trinity for the academic year 1883–1884, later extended to 1885.

No member of the royal family had any knowledge of the emotional upsets that plagued J. K.'s family. What they saw was an intelligent, attractive, witty and apparently earnest young scholar capable of getting Eddy through the basic elements of the university curriculum. What they did not see was a young man skilled in seducing people, rendering elusive statements and opinions, and most importantly, hiding his homosexuality. Like the Scarlet Pimpernel, J. K.'s gentlemanly disguise hid surprisingly deadly strengths.

As a tutor, J. K. must have spent many pleasant and delightful times at Sandringham, the royal residence in Norfolk. Within a short period, he established a tutorial system, using carefully screened undergraduates to participate in sharing information with the prince. The results were questionable.

J. K.'s tutoring was determined more from what was personally important for him than for Eddy or for the country. Interesting in this respect are Harrison's words: "Stephen, the ambitious member of an ambitious family, who had written in half-affectionate contempt that Eddy 'is a good-natured, unaffected youth, and disposed to exert himself to learn some history,' had soon discovered what interested Eddy."[14]

J. K. was both patronizing and prideful about his tutorial guidance of the prince. Conceivably, he had serious doubts about his pupil's ability to achieve. To that end he instituted an alternate plan, which began by his selecting certain companions for his charge. This displeased the prince's previous mentor, the Reverend John Dalton, who was not consulted in their selection. Rapidly, J. K. Stephen was becoming a significant force in Eddy's adult life and development, not only in his intellectual experiences, but also in his social and personal relationships.

Essentially, the Prince of Wales had granted J. K. *carte blanche* in facilitating Eddy's passage through the university, and J. K. laid his plans for himself as well as for Eddy. His intentions went far beyond his task of tutoring. From his association with the prince, he would eventually claim his own recognition and power.

One of the first men selected to be in the close circle around Eddy was H. F. (Harry) Wilson, a classmate of J. K.'s at Trinity College, who, along with J.K., would be destined for the law. Other associates were chosen, all brilliant scholars in their respective branches of learning.[15]

A photograph exists from this period of the prince surrounded by these "carefully selected friends." Vincent, in his authorized biography of Eddy, identifies each invaluable member of the group:

In the centre sits Prince Albert Victor, as broad and square in the shoulders as any of the constituent units of the group; on his left hand is Mr. H. L. Stephen (later Sir Herbert Stephen, Bart., Jem Stephen's elder brother), on his right is Mr. H. F. Wilson. Immediately behind the Prince stands Mr. J. K. Stephen, smothered in a soft white hat, not to be divorced from his indispensable pipe, with a cheery smile upon his face. Mounted high above Mr. Stephen, apparently sitting on his shoulders, is Mr. J. N. Langley. Reclining on the ground in front are Mr. Dalton (he was not yet a Canon of Windsor), Mr. J. W. Clark, and Mr. Goodhart (Harry Chester Goodhart, afterwards Professor of Latin at Edinburgh University; died 1895, aged 37); the remaining members of the group are Professor C. V. Stanford, Mr. A.H. Clough, Mr. F. B. Winthrop, Mr. J. D. Duff, Mr. A. H. Smith and Mr. H. B. Smith. By universal consent this fellowship of kindred spirits was one of the most delightful ever known; and those who have met many of the fellowship will not hesitate to say that it was an assembly of brilliant wits no less than of pleasant men.[16]

It is notable that no less than seven of those pictured were members of the Apostles.

Group picture at Cambridge. Queen Victoria's eldest grandson, Prince Albert Victor Christian Edward (Eddy) surrounded by his chosen friends. Seven members of the group were members of the University's most secret society, *The Apostles*. Note J. K. Stephen with pipe in mouth, seated behind Prince Eddy sporting a bowler hat.

As we have seen, J. K.'s outward appearance gave no hint of his homosexual proclivities, and in view of his close association with the prince, it was imperative that any such activities be concealed from public knowledge. Eddy's own sexual antics at the male brothels, as well as his close affiliation with the suspect Apostles, also fell short of socially acceptable behavior, and required cover-up.

As the heir apparent to the throne of England, Eddy had to be protected from public scandal at all costs. To some extent, J. K. was the royal family's last resort as a viable means of preparing the prince mentally for the task of kingship. It was an onerous, though impressive responsibility. The future leadership of Britain hinged upon the results of J. K.'s tutoring. It seems to me, however, that J. K. was more concerned with his own relationship with Eddy than with making a contribution to the British Empire. J. K.'s brother Herbert himself noted that "they [J. K. and Eddy] developed a firm relationship with each other."[17]

We will have reason to come back to this conclusion.

Entangled relationships often terminate in misery. The outcome of the relationship between J. K. Stephen and Eddy could be anticipated from its beginning. Let us see what happened during and after the years at Cambridge.

After his entrance into the university, Eddy's first interest was to join a number of clubs, following in his father's footsteps. The Prince of Wales had attended Cambridge also, but had not been permitted to live in college because his parents feared he might make undesirable acquaintances there. Royal princes were not expected to do any serious studying—least of all, the backward Eddy—and to avoid any possible embarrassments they were not asked to take examinations.

During his two years as a student at Trinity College, from 1883 to 1885, Eddy and his tutor occupied two sets of rooms in Neville's Court, which were termed the "Cambridge attics."[18] Taking an immediate interest in the social aspects of university life, the prince became a member of the Amateur Dramatic Club, through the sponsorship of J. K. Eddy purportedly liked music and had a Bluthner piano installed at the ADC's theater, which was used for concert performances. But Eddy himself did not play the piano.

For the most part, as we have seen, Eddy's Cambridge friends were handpicked by J. K. The latter had a close circle of intimates, whom he could rely on not to interfere with his possessive interest in his charge. One of the members of this circle was Herbert Stephen, J. K.'s older brother, who was an acknowledged whist player. According to Harrison, J. K. introduced Eddy to the game of whist, which kept the prince quite busy. Eddy was said to be a brilliant player, but I find that hard to comprehend, since whist, like bridge, is a game that requires concentration and attention— qualities sorely lacking in the heir apparent.

It was J. K.'s objective to restrict the prince's social acquaintances. Recognizing Eddy's homosexual propensities, J. K. designed an environment to encourage a homosexual relationship between him and the prince. A homosexual person does not need to be told who is or is not homosexual; he or she has an instinctive ability to recognize other people's sexual tendencies. Heterosexuals, generally speaking, do not possess such instinctive responses.

Michael Harrison in his book described Eddy as a "panerotic,"[19] whatever he meant by that term. Possibly, he meant that Eddy was oversexed—kept busy with thoughts, feelings and fantasies about sex. We have already established that the prince was emotionally and sexually immature. In such a regressed situation, he would have been curious about sex, but could not transfer his feelings into normal sexual desire for a woman. With J. K. now assuming the role of Eddy's mother, dominating him as his tutor and loving friend, Eddy probably fell easily into his comfortable, passive role as the submissive partner in such a relationship.

As time passed, there is reason to believe that the close nexus between the two developed into a real love relationship, with J. K. playing the dominant role. To some, it might appear that Eddy was a reluctant partner. History reported that when he was later discovered in the male brothel at Cleveland Street, he claimed that he came there only because he was curious. It is an unconvincing reason. It is more reasonable to believe that he actively enjoyed the company of homosexuals.

Both men were reared in a family background of competition and unrest. While J. K. was haunted by the absence of his mother, Eddy had a gallivanting father whose mind was more on his own pleasures than on his family. Both situations resulted in distorted sexual identification and low self-esteem.

Eddy revered J. K. as a gifted and witty scholar with a Cambridge degree; J. K. regarded Eddy as an attractive, effeminate young man on whom he could exert influence and power. Both shared miseries in their home lives and a dislike of women. Although each exhibited a manly facade, neither was emotionally able to love a woman. It was natural that they should feel an attraction for each other. But their relationship had to be kept secret. Nobody could know of their closeness. Eddy played a careful game of love with J. K. because he knew he was in the public eye. And the tutor kept a watchful and possessive guard upon the prince, because of his jealous, egocentric nature.

Though J. K. made every effort to hide his homosexual tendencies, there were suspicions about him. According to Harrison, an obscene song was circulating in Cambridge about this time, almost certainly written about J. K., that referred to a "Bastard Stephen" and seems to link both J. K. and Eddy in some supposed sexual scandal. Though elusive, its existence points subtly to a relationship between J. K. and the prince.[20]

After leaving Cambridge, Eddy became increasingly involved in public affairs and the relationship between him and J. K. seemed, on the surface, to have become more distant. Then in the winter of 1886–87, J. K. accidentally received a very severe blow on the head while he was on a visit to Felixstowe. Though he seemed to recover completely, his family and friends believed it colored his behavior for the remainder of his life. There are varying accounts of how the accident occurred.

According to A. C. Benson:

> There was an erection over a well, a pumping-mill, worked by a small windwheel. Jem Stephen clambered up the ladder to examine it, and either by accident or in attempting to take hold of the revolving sails, received a blow to his head which half stunned him.[21]

Another report stated that "the young man had an accident in which he damaged his head, and although the hurt did not appear to be serious it was in fact final and he began to go mad."[22]

Harrison reports that J. K. was carried, unconscious, into the millhouse, where he was treated by a local physician, and that he was then taken to his father's home at 32 De Vere Gardens, where he was further examined by Sir William Gull.[23]

Benson reported the finding of "some subtle inflammation of brain tissue."[24]

My own view is that J. K. was periodically manic depressive, with an abnormal and impulsive mind. It is quite possible, therefore, that he scaled the windmill to find out how the mechanism worked. It is extremely questionable that he was made mad by the ensuing accident. It is important to point out, however, that his behavior in acting so impulsively was like that of a child or an emotionally immature person with defective judgment—characteristic, in effect, of a person with possibly psychotic tendencies.

J. K.'s brother Herbert said of the accident: "He was badly cut. The wound healed, but I do not think he ever enjoyed perfect health again."[25]

A large part of J. K.'s continuing ill health, I believe, could be attributed to his feelings about Eddy, who was becoming increasingly preoccupied with his official duties. He had been made a Freeman of the City of London, and his name often appeared in the newspapers as a royal participant at various celebrations and dinners.[26] As the years passed, Eddy seemed to be drifting farther away.

It is conclusively established, nevertheless, that Eddy did keep in touch with his former college associates. A few of his letters are extant—all apparently innocuous, mentioning only daily happenings. All are written to H. F. (Harry) Wilson, J. K.'s close friend who had become Eddy's good friend at Cambridge. The lack of letters to J. K. is less surprising when we consider the need to cover up Eddy's intimate relationship with his former tutor. There is little doubt, however, that Eddy was greatly concerned upon learning of J. K.'s accident.

On June 8, 1888, Harrison tells us, Eddy went to Cambridge to receive the degree of LL.D., *Honoris Causa.* Harry Wilson did not attend the ceremony, but "he dutifully sent Eddy one of his poems."[27] On July 18, 1888, Eddy was admitted as a Knight of Justice in the Order of St. John of Jerusalem, and then visited the ancient city of York.

While Eddy was making these official appearances, where was J. K.? Following his accident in 1886, A. C. Benson wrote, J. K. "began to form sanguine and unbalanced plans, to be extravagant in money matters, and to display emotional tendencies of a rather vehement type."[28]

In 1888, J. K. started a journal called *The Reflector*, which, according to Benson, "was meant to be a concentration of sensible and well-informed journalism. He worked at it with immense energy and gusto and secured a band of very distinguished contributors, which included such names as Leslie Stephen, George Meredith, Mr. Birell, Mr. Anstey, Mr. Edmund Gosse, Mr. Bernard Holland, Lady Ritchie and Miss Mary Cholmondelay. Each number contained only one or two articles, and it was designed to supply a dependable and lively criticism of current thought and literature."[29] Benson noted, however, that the venture, begun on very insufficient capital, had never achieved a circulation of more than two hundred and fifty and that "after seventeen numbers the resources were exhausted."[30]

The failure of J. K.'s enterprise in journalism was a great disappointment to him; still more humiliating was the fact that his father had to pay the bills. Using his father's influence, J. K. obtained a legal clerkship that paid a stipend for light circuit duties, but he never worked at it; an assistant performed all the duties.[31]

Instead, J. K. "took up music and painting. He painted watercolour pictures of the most grotesque kind which he assured me were portraits," wrote A. C. Benson. "One in particular was of a female figure in a long brown coat sitting on the rail of a stile, in a kind of twilight, with a low moon in the distance. There was a curious suggestiveness about it. To me it would seem as though the female figure might be half-woman, half-man."[32]

In my opinion, J. K. painted the figure the way he felt he was— half of a human being.

Benson continues his report of J. K.: "His conversation was still so forcible and brilliant, that it [his behavior] was all put down to nothing more than the vagari of an original mind."[33]

Stephen's mental condition was far more than a vagary—it was a state of mind that the people who surrounded him did not grasp. I can safely state that J. K. had suffered serious mental illness since childhood; now he began to show signs of mental disintegration. It was becoming clear that he could no longer cope. Wrote Benson: "One can feel that he is a person who for too long a time has been under considerable stress and strain."[34]

J. K.'s frustrations and disappointments had reached their peak. He fought heroically to keep his emotional life under control, but the tension showed in both his speaking and writing. I believe that his sense of rejection by his lover and friend was also taking its toll.

Over the years, J. K. had written down his feelings and fantasies in poems, which he now published, as we have seen, under the title *Lapsus Calami*.[35] Even this title can be interpreted as indicative of gloom and foreboding. It means something lost by mistake, a slip of the tongue, pen, or memory, or a slip of the knife.

On the surface, the poems were innocent light verse. Beneath the clever constructions, however, the trained eye can perceive hostile and hateful emotions toward women, reflecting J. K.'s own experiences.

Many of the phrases in the poem "To A.T.M." allude to various aspects of J. K.'s homosexual behavior. Such detailed images as "a peppermint as schoolboys love," "Suck: and the less thou likest it the better," "Suck for our sake, and utter no complaint" are indications of J. K.'s experience and knowledge of homosexual practices. We can now understand the reason for his playful status among the young Etonians.

In my opinion, it was J. K.'s relationship, or his lack of a relationship, with his mother that initiated his frustration and disappointment and laid the foundation of his hatred for women. Such ambivalence is a common thread among homosexuals, who often vent their hostility against their mothers while unconsciously harboring a consuming desire for their love. In a poem entitled "A Thought," J. K. expresses a pathological dislike of women.

A THOUGHT

If all the harm that women have done
Were put in a bundle and rolled into one,
Earth would not hold it,
The sky could not enfold it,
It could not be lighted nor warmed by the sun;
Such masses of evil
Would puzzle the devil
And keep him in fuel while Time's wheels run.

But if all the harm that's been done by men
Were doubled and doubled and doubled again,
And melted and fused into vapour and then
Were squared and raised to the power of ten,
There wouldn't be nearly enough, not near,
To keep a small girl for the tenth of a year.

In another poem, "In the Backs," he spews forth totally inappropriate fury against a woman he sees while "strolling lonely in the Backs [the college gardens that border the River Cam]," describing her as "devoid of taste or shape or character" as "she stalked her dull unthinking way."[36]

Although the poem refers to but one woman, it reveals the depth of the writer's prejudice against all women. In fact, careful reading exposes a highly distorted and disturbed mind.

In particular, the poem's conclusion befits the attitude of a Jack the Ripper:

> I should not mind
> If she were done away with, killed, or
> ploughed.
> She did not seem to serve a useful end:
> And certainly she was not beautiful.[37]

The term "ploughed" has significant connotations when interpreted as meaning the forceful breaking through or cutting of the woman's body.

It has occurred to me that Jack the Ripper may have performed anal intercourse with some of his victims. It is the type of intercourse practiced among homosexuals. In such a position, the murderer was strategically placed to strangle his victim into unconsciousness before completing the ritual of cutting her apart. To Jack the Ripper, the end result of murder superseded the importance of sex. He did not rape his victims. It was not to his liking. Instead, he substituted his knife for his own act of rape.

The Ripper murders were in step with the rhyme called "Kaphozelum." It was an obscene and pornographic popular ballad of the day with a repeating melody for each stanza that deals with the "Harlots of Jerusalem," and it was a fitting label for the whores who were his chosen subjects, living in a district chiefly inhabited by Jews. Some verses of the poem follow:

It was for her no fortune good,
That he should need to root his pud,
And chose her out of all the brood
Of Harlots of Jerusalem.

For though he paid his women well,
This syphilitic spawn of hell.
Struck down each year and tolled the bell
For ten Harlots of Jerusalem.[38]

Harrison asserted that "this is a sentiment which must have echoed in the dying rattles of Polly Nichols, Annie Chapman, Elizabeth Stride, Catherine Eddowes and Marie Jeanette Kelly, in the autumn of 1888."[39] The sentiment also seems to reverberate in the postcard sent by Jack the Ripper to the Central News Agency, wherein he says, "I am down on whores and I shan't quit ripping them till I get buckled."[40]

In my opinion, J. K. was the man the witness Schwartz described at the scene of Elizabeth Stride's murder smoking a pipe. Harrison notes that photographs of J. K. consistently portrayed him "not to be divorced from his indispensable pipe."[41] With this in mind, I wondered whether J. K. had written about his pipe—and in *Lapsus Calami* I found a poem entitled "The Grand Old Pipe." In it, he describes his pipe as "my one consolation" which "keeps its hold on my favour."[42]

In order to link J. K. Stephen with the Ripper murders, I had to solve another important problem: How could J. K. have traveled from Cambridge to London, some fifty-four miles, in such short time, and without being discovered?

Comparing the days of the murders with J. K.'s schedule at Cambridge, where he was resident during the 1888 fall term as a fellow of King's College, I discovered the following:[43]

August 31, Mary Ann Nichols—Cambridge vacation.
September 8, Annie Chapman—Cambridge vacation.

September 30, Elizabeth Stride and Catherine Eddowes—
Michaelmas Term began the following day, October 1.

November 9, Marie Jeanette Kelly—halfterm holiday.

Each of the murders occurred during a hiatus in the university
term, when J.K. would probably have been visiting his home in
Kensington. The underground railway had been in operation since
1872. The trains stopped at Kensington High Street station, only
a short distance from Judge Stephen's house at 32 De Vere Gardens, Kensington, and went directly to Whitechapel.[44] It was
possible, therefore, for J.K. to have been at his parents' house and
to have reached the East End in little over half an hour.

We have revealed *who* the murderers were. But *why* would they
commit such horrendous crimes? The answers continually draw us
back to the psychological undertones of their personalities. In
J. K.'s case, the blow to his head might have worsened his mental
condition, but we know that he had shown symptoms of serious
mental disturbances with temper tantrums since childhood, and
all kinds of eccentricities combined with depressive and typically
aggressive manic behavior. The fact that Eddy seemed to have
become so busily occupied with public duties might have tipped
the scales in J. K.'s innately possessive and far from stable mind.
He would have been almost forced to confront his friend and lover
with the Apostolic view that the love of man was greater than love
for woman, whose sexual activities were inherently evil.

In his confused mind J. K. was convinced that women were
depraved, and that whores, and especially old whores, deserved to
be wiped out. It would not be difficult to persuade Eddy to join him
in committing the murders for mankind in the fall of 1888. So
began the onslaught of two men, each muddled in his own egocentricity, prowling the streets of Whitechapel in search of victims on
whom they would vent their accumulated frustration and hate.

The last of the Whitechapel victims was Marie Jeanette Kelly,
whose murder was the most gruesome of the five. According to the

evidence at her inquest, she was reportedly seen alive by a friend, Caroline Maxwell, the morning after her body had been found. We will examine how that was possible in the next chapter.

George Hutchinson did not appear at Kelly's inquest but his testimony was presented to and later reported by Abberline and Arnold at the denouement of the inquest as follows:

A number of witnesses were called who clearly established the identity of deceased. The coroner remarked that in his opinion it was unnecessary to adjourn the inquiry and the jury returned a verdict of willful murder against some person or persons unknown. [45]

They then discuss George Hutchinson:

An important statement has been made by a man named George Hutchinson which I forward herewith. I have interrogated him this evening and I am of opinion his statement is true. He informed me that he had occasionally given the deceased a few shillings, and that he had known her about 3 years. Also that he was surprised to see a man so well dressed in her company which caused him to watch them. He can identify the man and arrangement was at once made for two officers to accompany him round the district for a few hours tonight with a view of finding the man if possible.

Hutchinson is at present in no regular employment, and he has promised to go with an officer tomorrow morning at 11:30 A.M. to the Shoreditch Mortuary to identify the deceased. Several arrests have been made on suspicion of being connected with the recent murders, but the various persons detained have been able to satisfactorily account for their movements and were released.

F. G. Abberline, Inspector
J. Arnold, Superintendent[46]

Hutchinson's statement, recorded at the Commercial Street Police Station on November 12, 1888, was as follows:

161

Description age about 34 or 35. height 5 ft. 6. Complexion pale. dark eyes and eyelashes slight moustache. curled up each end. and hair dark. very surley looking dress long. dark coat. collar and cuffs trimmed astracan. and a dark jacket under. light waistcoat dark trousers dark felt hat turned down in the middle button boots and gaiters. with white buttons. wore a very thick gold chain. white linen collar. black tie. with horseshoe pin. respectable appearance

Geo Hutchinson[47]

Distinct items in the description turn our attention to Eddy. In fact, a family photograph shows Prince Eddy in the middle front seat wearing his button boots and gaiters with white buttons.[48]

The coroner terminated the inquest, even though there was testimony by a credible witness that gave several distinguishing characteristics of a man who might have been the murderer. What stopped the police from commencing an intensive search for the man described by Hutchinson? What more did they need to know?

It was now November and the perpetrator of at least five brutal murders had been at large since August 31, the date of the attack on Mary Anne Nichols. Many arrests and interrogations had led nowhere. Though the police, the Home Office and Scotland Yard faced constant public pressure, once again there was a failure to follow through effectively on the information of a credible witness.

Was it because the police had tired of playing the game of cat and mouse? Why not follow up on the whereabouts of the well-dressed man with a slight moustache and the astrakhan-trimmed coat? Was there concern about the consequences of capturing the man of "respectable appearance"?

Why should the police stop their investigations at the point when they were armed with such a detailed description of a suspect? Inspector Abberline agreed that Hutchinson was an honest witness; yet he failed to use his new and seemingly important information. Would such an arrest create even worse havoc for the people of the country?

Our plates are filled with questions, but there are not enough answers to satisfy our appetites. We pose this inquiry a hundred years too late, when there is no one left to respond to it. We can only think about who was being protected; we do know, however, that there were two men involved in the murders, and that the capture of one would undoubtedly lead to the capture of the other.

1. James Edmund Vincent, *His Royal Highness the Duke of Clarence and Avondale. A Memoir*, Murray, London, 1893, p. 137.
2. Michael Harrison, *Clarence, The Life of H. R. H. the Duke of Clarence and Avondale*, W. H. Allen, London, 1972, p. 30.
3. James Vincent, *op. cit.*, pp. 18–19.
4. Georgina Battiscombe, *Queen Alexandra*, Houghton Mifflin Company, Boston, 1969, p. 68.
5. Theo Aronson, *The King in Love*, Harper & Row, New York, 1988, p. 16.
6. Michael Harrison, *op. cit.*, p. 66.
7. Louise Clark, *How to Recognize and Overcome Dyslexia in Your Child*, Introduction, Archie A. Silver, M.D., *Dagbladeb*, Oslo, September 18, 1990.
8. Michael Harrison, *op. cit.*, p. 67.
9. *Ibid.*
10. *Ibid.*
11. James Vincent, *op. cit.*, p. 39.
12. John Van Der Kiste, *Edward VII's Children*, Allan Sutton, London, 1989, p. 49.
13. *Ibid.*
14. Michael Harrison, *op. cit.*, p. 94.
15. *Ibid.*, p. 85.
16. James Vincent, *op. cit.*, p. 85.
17. Herbert Stephen, *Complete and Final Edition of all J. K. Stephen's Poems*, Putnam & Sons, London, p. 6.
18. Arthur Christopher Benson, *The Leaves of the Tree. Studies in Biography*, G. P. Putnam's Sons, New York/London, 1911, pp. viii–ix.
19. Michael Harrison, *op. cit.*, pp. 115–116.
20. *Ibid.*

21. *Ibid.*
22. Quentin Bell, *Virginia Woolf: A Biography*, Harcourt Brace Jovanovich, New York, 1979, p. 35.
23. Michael Harrison, *op. cit.*, p. 126.
24. Arthur Benson, *op. cit.*, p. ix.
25. *Ibid.*
26. Michael Harrison, *op. cit.*
27. *Ibid.*, p. 131.
28. Arthur Benson, *op. cit.*, p. 135.
29. *Ibid.*
30. *Ibid.*, pp. 135–136.
31. *Ibid.*, p. 136.
32. *Ibid.*, pp. 136–137.
33. *Ibid.*, p. 137.
34. *Ibid.*
35. J. K. Stephen, *Lapsus Calami*, Macmillan & Bowes, Cambridge, 1891.
36. *Ibid.*, pp. 10–11.
37. *Ibid.*, p. 87, and *Cambridge Review*, February, 1891.
38. Michael Harrison, *op. cit.*
39. *Ibid.*, p. 173.
40. *Ibid.*, p. 32.
41. *Ibid.*, p. 85.
42. J. K. Stephen, *op. cit.*, pp. 8–9, and *Reflector*, January, 1888.
43. Anthony D. Haslam, *James Kenneth Stephen*, unpublished report, July 16, 1986, p. 4.
44. Information from London Underground Train System (September, 1988).
45. Report by Inspectors Abberline and Arnold, *Whitechapel Murders*, Metropolitan Police, November 12, 1888.
46. *Ibid.*
47. Report by George Hutchinson, Inquest, Metropolitan Police, November 12, 1888.
48. Theo Aronson, *op. cit.*

CHAPTER EIGHT

Secret Ties in Life and Death

"A mask tells us more than a face. These disguises intensify his personality, in that they concentrate his intentions."

OSCAR WILDE,
Pen, Pencil and Poison

IN NOVEMBER 1970, Dr. Thomas Stowell published his sensational article in *The Criminologist*. For the first time, he brought out evidence that seemed to verify what had earlier been talked about—that Prince Eddy had been involved in the Ripper murders. [1]

After recounting the series of five murders and analyzing them in detail, Stowell goes on to suggest that Sir Charles Warren and the police were primarily bent on preventing further murders and secondarily on suppressing the identification of "the heir of a noble and prominent family." [2] Clearly, the murderer was a lunatic and was not responsible for his actions. Stowell never identifies his suspect, whom he calls simply "S," but it is clear from his extensive listing of characteristics and attributes that Prince Eddy is the man in question. We will analyze these in more detail as we proceed through the chapter.

After identifying Sir William Gull as physician to the Queen and "a large number of the aristocracy and the wealthy including,

165

if I am right in my deductions, the family of Jack the Ripper," Stowell disposes of the rumors that Gull had been seen in White-chapel on nights when there had been murders by suggesting that he was probably there "for the purpose of certifying the murderer to be insane so that he might be put under restraint."[3]

The source of Stowell's theory appears to be chiefly information provided to him personally by Gull's daughter, Caroline, who was married to Theodore Dyke Acland, M.D., F.R.C.P. Unfortunately, the research on which he based his theory was chiefly in the form of oral confidences—the Aclands had been good friends with Dr. Stowell for many years—and when Stowell died soon after his article was published, his daughter destroyed the notes on which he had based it.

According to Stowell:

Mrs. Acland's story was that at the time of the Ripper murders, her mother, Lady Gull, was greatly annoyed one night by an unappointed visit from a police officer, accompanied by a man who called himself a "medium." [This was obviously the medium named Lees, who had been helping the police with their inquiries.] She was irritated by their impudence in asking her a number of questions which seemed to her impertinent. She answered the questions with noncommittal replies such as "I do not know," "I cannot tell you that," "I am afraid I cannot answer that question."

Later Sir William himself came down and in answer to the questions said he occasionally suffered from lapses of memory since he had had a slight stroke in 1887; he said that he had once discovered blood on his shirt. This is not surprising if he had medically examined the Ripper after one of his murders.[4]

The article continues:

Jack the Ripper was obviously Sir William Gull's patient. Mrs. Acland told me she had seen in her father's diary an entry, "I informed _____ that his son was dying of syphilis of the brain." The date of the entry was November 1889, after "S" had returned from his recuperative voyage. Evidently toward the end of 1889 "S" had another relapse which caused Sir William Gull to make his sad and gloomy but accurate prognosis. The patient did not recover but passed into the inevitable stage in which he was unaware of place and time, recognizing no one; he died little more than a year later.[5]

Dr. Stowell adds that there was "evidence that 'S' was the scion of a noble house, heir to an illustrious title and great wealth. He was under medium height and had a fair moustache and wore a deerstalker hat in which to commit his acts of raving lunacy . . . With his father's friends he stalked deer on the family estate in Scotland. This gave him many opportunities of watching the dressing of the carcasses, and if he wished, of assisting in the operation. In doing this he would have learned how to remove bowels, kidney, liver, heart, lungs and uterus neatly."[6]

Those persons with a disordered sexual personality, described today as a sexual psychopath, becomes sexually aroused by watching eviscerations and mutilations. "S"'s syphilitic infection could have led to a psychotic condition that would have contributed to his participation in the murders.

It was Dr. Stowell's observations that finally brought to light the evidence linking Prince Eddy with the Whitechapel murders. Unquestionably, the prince was the scion of a noble house, heir to an illustrious title and wealth, under medium height, with a fair moustache, and known to stalk animals on a Scottish family estate. A photograph of Eddy shows him dressed for fishing and wearing a deerstalker hat.

Dr. Stowell's theory is that "S" had become infected with syphilis at the age of nineteen at "one of the many shore parties he had enjoyed in the West Indies on his world journey."[7]

167

This photo, titled "Fishing," was actually a studio portrait of Prince Eddy wearing his high "collar and cuffs." Circa 1890.

He continues:

Some six weeks later he had an important public appointment in what was then one of our Colonies. At the last moment he canceled that appointment on account of a "trifling ailment." The abandonment of an important engagement on account of a trifling ailment is unusual unless it is causing severe pain or obvious disfigurement, e.g. toothache or the development of visible rash.[8]

Stowell believes that the "trifling ailment" could well have been the appearance of the skin rash of secondary syphilis, appearing six weeks after the primary infection "S" had contracted in the Caribbean. "As to whether this was recognized and adequately treated," he adds somberly, "I have some misgivings in the light of later events."9

I share Dr. Stowell's doubts that Eddy's ailment was properly treated during his tour of the colonies, and join him in condemning the rather ignorant conclusion that Eddy had no real excuse for canceling his appointment. Had Dr. William Gull examined him, he would have been well aware that his patient required immediate treatment. And in fact, on Eddy's return from his round-the-world tour on the ship *Backhand* in 1878–1881, Gull is known to have treated him with iodine, which was a medication used at that time against syphilis.

Stowell's theory depended on some further information, presumably also obtained from Mrs. Acland, according to which Sir William Gull had had the suspect certified to be insane (one of the signs of increasing syphilis) and committed to a private home for the mentally ill not far from London, where he remained under restraint until November 9, when he managed to escape to Whitechapel and commit the atrocious murder of Marie Jeanette Kelly—after which he was again picked up by Sir William Gull and readmitted to the home.

This scenario could explain the unusually long interval between the fourth and fifth murders—a gap of forty days, instead of the usual fourteen, before the murderer struck again.

It is certainly significant, as Stowell points out, that after the murder of Marie Jeanette Kelly on November 9, the police relaxed their vigilance. The senior inspectors assigned to Whitechapel were withdrawn, as were the constables who had been sent there, and the special patrols were disbanded. We can echo Dr. Stowell's question: "Did they know with certainty that the murderer was again restrained, far away from the possibility of continuing his career of mutilation?"10

Although there are a great many reasons to suppose that the evidence adduced by Stowell refers directly to Eddy, I think that he was the secondary player in this appalling drama masterminded by J. K.

The "firm friendship" between the prince and his former tutor, J. K. Stephen, may appear on the surface to have cooled somewhat, but I believe it was quite the reverse. The fact that no letters survive that they wrote to each other does not mean that none were written. I also postulate that some of Eddy's emotional and intellectual slowness was due to dyslexia, and that he probably preferred to dictate letters to an aide (a common practice at that time). That, too, would have hindered his expression of anything personal or intimate, even in his communications to J. K. indirectly through such friends as Harry Wilson.

We have previously shown that two men, whom I identify as J. K. and Eddy, had been present at the murder scenes of the third, fourth and fifth victims. Stowell interpreted the description of a person wearing the deerstalker hat, as a characteristic of "S" when dressed to kill. [11]

Both men had the emotional desire and ability to kill, and J. K. united their forces of motivation. We have also shown that an intimate relationship existed between the two, which, because of its homosexual nature, had to be kept secret. When Eddy first left Cambridge, J. K. was still able to keep Eddy under his domination, and it is a fair assumption that they saw much more of each other than was realized. However, as Eddy became increasingly involved in public life, J. K. felt his influence diminishing and he grew insanely jealous—to the point of deciding to perform feats that would link Eddy to him permanently. He desperately needed to get Eddy back and show his power to him, as a hero.

Nobody actually witnessed any of the killings. But from our findings and knowledge of mass murderers we can conclude that before they could find a victim the murderers had to investigate the terrain. They both became hunters, which was much to their liking, and in stalking their victims they became well acquainted with the London streets. One or both knew of the water basin half hidden and located back from the street, where they paused to wash the blood from their hands. [12]

Both had it in mind that women, and in particular prostitutes, deserved to be killed. I doubt whether J. K. needed to use much persuasion to get Eddy, who loved to hunt and kill, to join him in wiping out these women they jointly found so threatening. His manic and episodic moods, which he could barely control, increased his naturally jealous, possessive temperament and demanded direct, exciting action of a kind that would stir the world. And Eddy, whose syphilis was advancing into the typical phase of the onset of insanity, was an ideal accomplice. It seems reasonable to think that the two men met at J. K.'s parents' home and from there took the underground railway from Kensington directly to Whitechapel. The trip took less than an hour, and around 10:00 or 11:00 P.M. they were ready to start their hunting. Previous investigators have been inclined to believe that the murderer took a hansom cab. It seems to me far more effective to use the underground train, which could bring them quickly to Whitechapel and back without being discovered by anyone, while the police were scrambling to find the murderers. Both had probably participated in gralloching (removing the entrails of) dead animals on the moors, and I believe it mattered little to them whether the body was that of an animal or a woman.

They were not always successful in snaring an easy prey. In some cases, they would have approached other prostitutes, but been rejected. And after the murder of Stride, the murderer had to beat a hasty retreat when warned by his partner of impending discovery. But then, as mentioned, he caught up with Catherine Eddowes in the City and made her his fourth victim. After that fourth killing, however, Sir William Gull put Eddy into the private mental home and kept him there until November 9, when he escaped.

According to this scenario, he would have gone straight to J. K. and the two would have boarded the train to Whitechapel. But it took time before they found a prostitute willing to go with them. It was around 1:00 A.M. that Eddy encountered Marie Jeanette Kelly and persuaded her to take him, and possibly J. K. too, to her room—and her undoing. Approaching Kelly as a pair may have thrown off any suspicion by Marie that she had run into Jack the Ripper.

How did it happen that Marie Jeanette Kelly was said to have been seen the morning after she had been found brutally murdered?

Following the murder, about 4:00 A.M., a fire was set in the grate of Kelly's room, which lasted for fully half an hour. One man left the building about 6:00 A.M., and was heard walking away. The door was locked behind him.

J. K. and Eddy may well have put on women's clothes at some stage in the mutilation of Kelly's body, as part of the gruesome ritual, then lit a fire in order to get rid of their bloody garments—a fire so hot that it melted the kettle. There were extra clothes in the room that had been left by a woman friend. Perhaps they brought their own women's garments, or at least underclothes with them. Many homosexuals carry and/or wear women's underwear, particularly when having sexual intercourse. Women's underwear stimulates sexual orgasm.

I suggest that they decided a disguise in women's clothes would be ingenious, and that—possibly helped by J.K. before he walked away down the passage between 5:00 and 6:00 A.M.—Eddy put on Marie's dress and shawl, shaving off his moustache and taking pains and time to create a convincing replica of the victim. Leaving the room, he carefully closed and locked the door after him in order to delay the discovery of the mutilated body and to allow ample time for his escape. Dressed like Marie, he played the role of a transvestite, a frequent homosexual pattern of behavior, with a success that was measured by the encounter with Mrs. Maxwell between 8:00 and 8:30 that morning.

There were two stumbling blocks in this reasoning. One was found in Mrs. Maxwell's testimony. If, indeed, Marie Jeanette Kelly had addressed her by name, the masquerade by Eddy would not be plausible. However, there was no corroboration of Maxwell's testimony and some doubts persisted in view of the discrepancies between her testimony and that of other witnesses. The personal interchange, therefore, may have been consciously or unconsciously fabricated by her to reinforce her statement that she saw the victim alive.

The other stumbling block was found in Inspector Abberline's testimony, in which he mentioned that articles of a woman's clothing were retrieved from the ashes. I have already accounted for this possibility by suggesting that the murderers donned women's clothes before or during the mutilation, burned them thereafter, and then redressed in other women's garments. In any event, however, I am not deterred by Abberline's statement. Scientific examinations were as yet too unsophisticated to decipher the embers of totally consumed objects. It is likely—even probable—that the murderers would destroy their male garments to prevent any link to them. The intense heat generated in the grate was sufficient to melt the spout on the kettle propped on the grate. It also may have been sufficient to render identification of the embers unreliable.

Such behavior may seem farfetched to a lay person, but it is commonplace to a well-trained psychiatrist or psychoanalyst. To see how effectively certain homosexual men can imitate and transform themselves into beautiful, appealing women, one need only visit certain gay bars. These "ladies" often go undetected by the heterosexual eye and reveal their masculine origins only through their manly voices. And Eddy's was rather high-pitched. Sufficiently so, it even may have been, to deceive Mrs. Maxwell on the other side of the street.

No sane men could have committed so atrocious an act. I believe the enormity of it sated and also scarred them both permanently. According to Howells and Skinner and Stowell, Sir William Gull must have been on the lookout for Eddy and found him quite speedily, despite his disguise, maybe because he was acting in

173

an obviously deranged fashion. Following a fresh sojourn in the asylum, careful nursing and good care restored him, for a while, and he was able to resume at least some of his royal duties and appear to be in good health. J.K., as we shall see later, was not so fortunate.

Prince Eddy's private activities gained notoriety among the citizenry; yet there was no public denial of his antics. In such a climate of opinion, is it any wonder that the conviction grew that the police must have concealed evidence about the Whitechapel murders?

Nearly a year after the rampage began, in July 1889, Prince Eddy was reported seen in the famous male brothel at 19 Cleveland Street. Lord Arthur Somerset, Eddy's friend and superintendent of the royal family's stables, had been found in the company of a telegraph boy. Although the prince had escaped arrest during a police raid, Howells and Skinner report that "Prince Albert Victor certainly was in the Department of Public Prosecutions file on alleged patrons—he was referred to as P.A.V."[13]

The Cleveland Street scandal posed considerable problems for the royal family. In view of the gossip about Eddy's activities, the Prince and Princess of Wales resolved that it would be best if their son were removed temporarily from public view and the reach of the newspapers. So in the fall of 1889 they sent him to India.

The visit was carefully planned and supervised. The prince's companion on the trip was Sir Edward Bradford, V.C., who later became Chief Commissioner of the Metropolitan Police. I interpret this to mean that the family suspected the prince of being involved in some really serious trouble, and took precautions against any chances of further misconduct.

The version of Eddy's visit to India found in James Edmund Vincent's *Memoir* gives a vivid, although highly censored description of his stay. The streets of the cities he visited were lined with troops, and dinner parties were held in his honor, all giving the impression that the visit was a matter of serious official business.

Closer reading, however, shows that Eddy spent most of his time in one of his most absorbing pastimes—hunting. Like many other members of his family, he was more interested in the outdoor life than in political or intellectual pursuits. "As a horseman of a high order, as a shot of real brilliancy, having regard to his age," according to Vincent, "the Prince possessed two manly accomplishments calculated to endear him to a very large section of the British nation."[14]

On the Indian expedition in 1889, the chief recreation was shooting tigers, boars and bucks. When there was no opportunity to shoot, the prince used a spear. "We [Vincent and Eddy's entourage] beat through a large extent of long grass some four to five feet high," continues the indefatigable Vincent. "We moved a lot of pig but for some time no boars. At last one got up and we rode him a long distance till he lay down. H.R.H. then rode up and took a spear and we soon killed him."[15]

Quail shooting was also numbered among Eddy's skills. Vincent noted proudly that Eddy bagged two hundred and forty-eight pair in one day, "when we ran out of cartridges; I believe if we had worked hard we could have got five hundred couple."[16]

The Indian visit took its toll on Eddy. When he returned to London in May 1890, he looked haggard, pale and tired, and had lost a considerable amount of weight. His mother was immediately disquieted by his appearance. She began a new plan for his well-being—the time-honored solution all mothers proposed for their children's difficulties: marriage.

Modern-day experience has taught us that in some cases marriage may be the worst solution for a disturbed person's emotional health. Victorian culture, however, dictated such a union, especially for the eventual heir to the throne, who had just been honored with a new title: Duke of Clarence and Avondale.

Every account of Eddy's life reports that on his return to England he fell in love with the Princess Helene, daughter of the Comte de Paris, pretender to the French throne—who was a

175

Catholic. Eddy became engaged to Helene in August 1890, but the engagement was canceled within a year, ostensibly for religious reasons.[17] Claiming that he could never be happy without his betrothed, Eddy offered to abdicate his right to the throne, but unlike his yet-to-be born nephew, Edward VIII, he did not do so.

My professional opinion is that Eddy was never emotionally able to love a woman except for his mother. Even during his courtship of Helene, he claimed, "I now love two women."[18] He was emotionally oriented toward males for his sexual gratification. Nevertheless, in November 1891 he again made plans to marry— this time, his cousin, Princess May of Teck, who was both English and Protestant. The date was set for February 27, 1892—but the prince became seriously ill over Christmas and died just a few weeks before his wedding day.

The royal physician, Sir William Gull, was undoubtedly consulted about Eddy's apparent decline in health on his return from India. His morality was of the highest order; yet he was torn between his obligations to the Queen and the disclosure of his medical findings to the public. His decision to protect the monarch on another occasion was reported in Richard Gordon's book *Jack the Ripper*. According to Gordon, Gull referred to having found a scrofula (an open wound that has to be covered, a sign of tuberculosis) in Eddy's neck that was similar to a scrofula Princess Alexandra had had. "If the report shows scrofula," Gull is reported to have added somberly, "we doctors must lie for the good of our country, like diplomats."[19]

While Eddy was in India, how did J. K. spend his time? We can be sure of one thing—his private thoughts and feelings remained secret and guarded. He continued to teach at Cambridge and shielded his movements during the lengthy vacations. He was not as successful in completely covering up his erratic, manic-depressive behavior. Suspicion lingered that there was something wrong with him, and there were rumors that he had been seeking medical help. Where, with whom and when, he wanted to remain secret.

My research led me to St. Andrew's Hospital, Northampton, where J. K. was confined from November 1891 until his death a couple of months later. In the files, I found a memorandum marked "Private and Confidential," which initially made no sense to me. Then I realized that J. K. himself was the author of the memorandum. It was a mental evaluation written by him, the patient, as if it were being written about someone else. The tone of arrogance typifies a person with pronounced sexual and narcissistic personality disorders. J. K. was attempting to refute the existence of the emotional and mental illness that had gripped his life. But the more he strove to appear normal, the more obvious his abnormality became. His situation had become desperate and gloomy, reflecting the depressive phase of his illness. J. K. would not accept what had happened to him. The extent of J. K.'s fascinating self-deception warrants reprinting here for the reader's examination.[20]

PRIVATE AND CONFIDENTIAL.

About the end of October last Dr G. H. Savage, of 3, Henrietta Street, formerly Principal of Bedlam, formed the opinion that the gentleman hereinafter referred to was not in a state of perfect mental health, but was suffering from morbid excitement or cerebral exaltation. Dr Savage had some personal acquaintance with the gentleman in question and his past career; but the opinion in question was formed without personal examination, and indeed without seeing the patient.

The opinion of Dr Savage became known to many relations, friends and acquaintances of the object of his suspicion, and to the members of his club, with results of a damaging, if not disastrous character.

The gentleman was never medically examined by Dr Savage; but he was separately examined by Sir Andrew Clark, Dr Hughlings Jackson and Dr Hack Tuke in October, November and December. Sir Andrew Clark declared that he was in perfect physical health, and would continue so if he adopted certain regulations as to diet, clothing, &c., which he practically did.

Dr Hughlings Jackson was of opinion that his nervous system was in perfect order; he would give no opinion as to his brain.

Dr Hack Tuke, after a very prolonged and minute examination, could find no trace of brain disease; but was of opinion that Dr Savage was unlikely to go wrong on such a matter.

Early in January, 1891, the patient was examined at Paris by two eminent French doctors, who certified in writing that he was free from brain disease.

In December Dr Savage expressed the opinion that the patient ought to be put under restraint; and that, failing this, he ought to go to some quiet and distant place for several months, if possible under the close superintendence of a medical attendant. If this were not done he anticipated an outbreak of a serious, and probably violent, character. He especially deprecated staying in London, visiting Paris, or going to Cambridge.

In defiance of Dr Savage's advice his patient stayed in London, visited Paris, and went to Cambridge.

No serious or violent attack took place.

Dr Savage's patient has been, since January, at Cambridge and London. In the former place he has lived a busy and active life, seeing old friends, and making new ones; dispensing and receiving hospitality; reading, writing, speaking at public debates and political meetings, lecturing on law and coaching in history. He has contributed to newspapers, begun two books, and published a third. He has taken no advice, and subjected himself to no restraint.

During this time he has corresponded with Dr Savage, and has seen him when in London. At an interview in February Dr Savage expressed the opinion that he was much better, if not entirely recovered (despite his neglect of advice). Subsequently, after consultation with a friend of both parties resident at Cambridge, Dr Savage and Dr Hack Tuke wrote a joint opinion advising him to stay at Cambridge and go on with his work as a teacher.

In April Dr Savage, at an interview, admitted that his expectations had not come true; and that the defiance of his advice had not produced the expected evils. Upon the patient declaring that he believed he had never suffered from excitement or exaltation, or done anything he had cause to regret, Dr Savage said that this belief was a symptom of dormant disease, and a proof that the recovery was not perfect.

In November, 1890, Dr Savage wrote the following letter, which was sealed up and endorsed "not to be opened till May 1891." On the first of May the patient opened the letter, which ran as follows:

3, HENRIETTA STREET,
CAVENDISH SQUARE, W.
November 21, 1890

DEAR

According to promise I write my opinion as to the next 6 months of your life.

For some weeks to come there will be waste of money, buying useless things, i.e. things for which you have no real need.

You will borrow money right and left. You will dress in unconventional ways and cause worry to your relations.

You will discover that you have incurred debts which of yourself you cannot pay and will feel it a grievance that you have to fall in with the conditions which are imposed.

You will then take to bed and spend much of the spring in reading in bed and doing nothing of any good, not earning a living. The period will be one rather of exhaustion than of depression, and so the circle will be completed.

I am,

Yours truly

G. H. SAVAGE

During the first weeks above referred to, the patient bought nothing, borrowed nothing, and dressed conventionally. During the whole of the six months he rose early, worked hard, and earned

179

a fair income. He never made any discovery of debts which he could not pay.

Dr Savage has often expressed the opinion that his patient would not recover without first going through a prolonged period of depression or exhaustion. It is common ground between him and the patient that no such period has taken place.

Dr Savage says that, owing to peculiar circumstances for which he did not make allowance, his prophecy was not fulfilled: but he declares that his patient's present good health is temporary and that the prophecy will be fulfilled some day.

Dr Savage's opinions as to the future course of the disease were expressed, in November, in unqualified terms and with unbounded confidence.

Under these circumstances it is submitted that the opinion of Dr Savage on this case is absolutely worthless: and that there is no ground to suppose that the person referred to ever suffered from morbid excitement or exaltation.

This suggestion is made, in the interest of a person who has been gravely prejudiced, if not irreparably damaged, by an opinion formed in good faith, but, as he believes, on wholly erroneous grounds. It is not intended to depreciate Dr Savage's deservedly high reputation: but merely to imply that he has, in this case, made one of those mistakes from which the most eminent physicians cannot be wholly exempt.

CAMBRIDGE,
May, 1891.

In his relationship with Eddy, J. K., as was his wont, played the dominant role, and was well-suited for the part. He was highly intelligent, restless, manic-depressive, impulsive and aggressive. In contrast, Eddy was slow, dependent, impressionable, backward, listless and pliable. Through their differences, they drew closer, transcending their social strata and lifestyles. J. K. was a commoner, possessive and domineering, while Eddy, the royal prince, slipped comfortably into his passive role. To a sane man, the role

180

of tutor and guide to so malleable an heir to the throne would have been the opportunity of a lifetime for honor, prestige and power. But to J. K., on the edge of insanity, it became another game to achieve his self-centered desires.

His reasons for wanting to dominate far exceeded the objectives originally outlined in his tutorial mandate. Intellectual achievement for such a pupil as Eddy was, in any case, out of the question. Eventually, they shared a common base of feelings and what appeared to the untrained eye as great differences in their personality and character were in fact the makings of an emotional intermeshing—like a key in a lock.

We may surmise that J. K. strengthened Eddy's natural homosexual feelings. It is easy to imagine his passive, pliable personality under peer pressure from the strong, egocentric personality of J.K. But his submissive psyche was also easy prey to other influences from such sources as the Cambridge secret society, the Apostles, or the less defined but closely knit group of homosexual aristocrats involved in the Cleveland Street scandal.

It makes sense that J. K.'s homosexual advances would be clandestine, under the cloak of intellectual pursuits. Since such practices were strictly condemned and severely punished, secrecy became the watchword between the two. Nevertheless, rumors did circulate involving a relationship between them.

One one side, Sir William Gull kept the royal family from knowing the true extent of Eddy's illness. On another side, there must have been diligent efforts to smother the rumors that were rife about the Whitechapel murders and the connection between the prince and his former tutor.

On one occasion, Eddy returned to Cambridge in November 1890 and, according to Harrison, spent the last day of his visit there with J. K. J. K.'s father, Judge Fitzjames Stephen, was ill and Eddy's concern may have prompted the prince's social call. No report of the meeting exists, so we can only surmise what happened that day between the two men.[21]

A year later, in November 1891, J. K. Stephen learned, either directly or indirectly through correspondence from the prince, that Eddy was to marry Princess May of Teck. J. K. felt fury and frustration. In 1888, he had found an outlet for such feelings by taking bloody revenge on others. How could he take revenge now? His partner in love and crime had been rent from him, and it was too risky to act alone.

"It's too late, it's too late," he kept lamenting during his last days in the hospital.[22] All that remained of his extraordinary relationship with Eddy was the secret of their intimacy.

The thrill of the murders excited J. K.; then it depressed him with feelings of guilt. The admission report from St. Andrew's Hospital recorded that J. K. "thought that someone was after him," an important remark, indicating that he felt guilty about a criminal act he had performed.[23] We come closer to his confession in Virginia Woolf's impressions of her cousin J. K. during the period of gradual deterioration that preceded his final breakdown. She vividly portrays the tragedy of a gifted man gone insane. She remembered every detail of his deranged conduct, even after forty years:

. . . There were many young men, it seemed, when one dashed in for a second, sitting round Stella. [Stella Duckworth was Virginia's half-sister, the daughter of Julia, Lady Stephen, by her first marriage, who lived at Hyde Park Gate with the family, acting as what has been called "a household Cinderella" and family caretaker. She was aged about 20 at this time.] Vaguely we knew that Arthur Studd was in love with her; and Ted Sanderson; and I think Richard Norton; and Jem [J. K.] Stephen. That great figure with the deep voice and the wild eyes would come to the house looking for her, with his madness on him; and would burst into the nursery and spear the bread on his swordstick and at one time we were told to go out by the back door and if we met Jem we were to say that Stella was away.

. . . Jem Stephen was in love with Stella. He was mad then. He was in the exalted stage of his madness. He would dash up in a hansom; leave my father to pay it. The hansom had been driving him about London all day. The man wanted perhaps a sovereign. It was paid. For "dear Jem" was a great favourite. Once, as I say, he dashed up [to] the nursery and speared the bread. Another time, off we went to his room in De Vere Gardens and he painted me on a small bit of wood. He was a great painter for a time. I suppose madness made him believe he was all powerful. Once he came in at breakfast. "Savage [Dr. George Savage, later Sir George, an old friend of the Stephen family; it was he who committed J. K. to the Northampton Hospital. Later, he was Virginia's own specialist.] has just told me I'm in danger of dying or going mad," he laughed. And soon he ran naked through Cambridge; was taken to an asylum; and died. This great mad figure with his broad shoulders and very clean cut mouth, and the deep voice and the powerful face—and the very blue eyes—this mad man would recite poetry to us; "The Burial of Sir John Moore," I remember; and he always brings to mind some tormented bull; and also Achilles—Achilles on his pressed bed lolling roars out a deep applause. He was in love with Stella—incongruously enough. And we had orders to tell him, if we met him in the street, that she was away, staying with the Lushingtons at Pyports. There was a great mystery about love then.[24]

While writing about Stella, Virginia Woolf could not forget her own sexual experiences as a child. In her work she alludes to being fondled by certain family members, an experience we now characterize as sexual abuse. She explained in her prose that she did not tell the man to stop because she feared he would continue to assault her, which he did anyway. When she became sexually excited, she felt even more guilty and ashamed. The consequences of these feelings contributed to her depression and resultant attempts at suicide. Might one of the family members who fondled her also have been a perpetrator of the Whitechapel murders? The thought is a confounding one.

183

Virginia Woolf, circa 1925.

Louise De Salvo appears to clarify the question in her saga of Virginia Woolf:

> By the time she wrote this story [about the bull] Virginia had been abducted at least once by J. K. Stephen and she had experienced at least one incident of sexual violation that we know of. In her text, the narrator transmutes the bull with the erect tail first into a frightened calf running to the stream to drink and then to a cow. [25]

Although it may be difficult to determine the precise cause of a psychosis, I am skeptical that J. K.'s head trauma was the cause of his derangement, though the accident may have hastened its onset. There was a great deal of mental pathology throughout the line of his family members—father, uncle, cousin. A careful reading of his poems, as we have seen, reveals his hostility against women, despite his attempts to cloak the poems with lightness—

his usual subterfuge to divert attention from the intensity of his real feelings. His defense against depression was to cope with his life experiences humorously. But he thereby ran the danger of making his real life situation into a parody.

Like Puck, the evil sprite, full of mischief and mania, ever ready to play a game, J. K. played his game with life until reality overtook him. He had kept his real feelings secret for fear of public outrage and offense. Their intensity grew ever more burdensome as Eddy moved further out of his control and his life. It was natural he should feel cheated. He had been loyal to Eddy, had tried to show how much Eddy meant to him—much more than any woman. They had shared the excitement and challenge of a murderous game, along with the risk that their secret would be discovered and exposed.

The manner and style of the murders were laden with psychological overtones. J. K. and Eddy had, I believe, made a pact to activate their malice toward women. These feelings had been festering since their youth; the scheme was now ripe for action. Each in his own way had communicated his disdain for women, but so subtly camouflaged as to be discernible only to those with similar propensities. Murder would be the zenith of expression for such dislike. I see them as the forerunners of Leopold and Loeb in 1924, a conspiring couple of sophisticated criminals, plotting the details of their pending crimes right down to the choice of password. During their murders, they developed a warning signal in the word "Lipski," just as Leopold and Loeb had warned each other with the words "For Robert's sake."[26]

When J. K. reflected on how, thanks to his planning, he and his lover had dispelled their venom undisturbed and undiscovered, he likely shook with anger at Eddy for his ultimate betrayal—marriage. Had Eddy forsaken the principles of the Apostles' "higher sodomy" for the sexual attraction of a woman?[27]

I think that J. K. grew more and more preoccupied with the possible loss of Eddy's friendship and his dreams of being the power

185

behind the throne. Such visions went very well with his grandiose fantasies of unlimited success and power—which now would never materialize. Until the end, however, J. K. never gave up hope of regaining his relationship with Eddy. He had sacrificed for him before and was willing to do so again. He had even murdered to obtain the prince's respect and to ensure his dominant role in their relationship.

As close cronies, both men probably frequented the same social clubs and restaurants in London, a number of which were homosexual bars or brothels. These social excursions could have heightened J. K.'s jealousy. The threat of any potential competition in the relationship could have stirred the murderous assaults in Whitechapel.

Jealousy, as most psychiatrists will confirm, is more firmly and frequently rooted in homosexual persons than in heterosexual ones. Heterosexuals experience jealousy but its intensity among homosexuals is considerably higher, in part because of the relative scarcity of homosexual partners within the general population.

Within two years after the Whitechapel murders, J.K.'s mental aberrations, as we have seen, had become ever more apparent. And Eddy, too, was being treated by Gull upon his return from India, when he was on the downward path from the manic stage of syphilis to the depression and dementia that would finally overtake him. Dr. Thomas Stowell commented in his article that " 'S' was kept alive so long only by means of medical skill and unremitting careful nursing—in his father's country house."[28]

It is not clear whether Stowell was referring to J. K. or Eddy. Both men had become seriously ill and were under treatment during overlapping periods. Eddy began the final stages of illness and dementia at the end of December 1891; J. K.'s decline into severe depression, which had begun much earlier, had reached its low point in November 1891. Even in illness they were in lockstep with one another. Having shared a life of mutual emotional disturbances, now they would share a death of mental derangement.

The announcement of Eddy's marriage to Princess May played a dual role of not only convincing others, but also himself, of his manhood. The royal family, of course, reveled in the prospect that marriage would remove any residue of his mental or emotional instability. The outcome would never be known. On January 7, 1892, a month before his intended wedding, Eddy became fatally ill.

The previous day, January 6, the prince and a number of guests were engaged in shooting pheasants at Sandringham. Many of the guests were suffering from heavy colds and influenza and were forced to retire to their rooms. Eddy also had the flu, but he stuck to his shooting all day and returned in the evening to go to bed. Next day, after lunch, he was taken seriously ill with piercing abdominal pain and dizziness. By evening the pain had lessened and his fever had subsided.

The next morning, January 8, was his birthday. He felt well enough to get up and insisted on going downstairs to open his presents. But on January 9, his temperature soared again and he had a rattling cough.

A consulting physician, Dr. Francis Laking, diagnosed the illness as incipient pneumonia. He telegraphed Dr. W. H. Broadbent for further consultation. Broadbent arrived later in the day and examined Eddy. The patient was coherent and in good spirits—but then the prince's condition worsened.

His mind shifted in and out of consciousness, his cough was worse, and his breathing, short and painful, was enough to elicit cries and moans from him. That night he grew delirious. The next day he was heard shouting in fury at Lord Churchill and Lord Salisbury. [Neither one was present.] Then he called out wildly, "Helene, Helene." [Princess Helene of France, his first fiancée.] Pain overcame him and he lapsed into unconsciousness, only to return to consciousness moments later to cry out again.[29]

Eddy's agonizing struggle against death continued, with his "head rising stiffly from his pillows and falling back with piercing, unintelligible cries that were not usually symptomatic of pneumonia."[30]

No, indeed they were not. When I read this report, I instantly recognized the piercing abdominal pains as gastric crises of the type which are pathological for patients suffering from the third stage of neurosyphilis. In such a condition, abdominal pains come with suddenness and may last for hours. Just as suddenly, they disappear, which is further evidence of *tabes dorsalis*, a syphilitic condition. This illness may well have brought about Eddy's death.[31]

> Eddy's death struggle lasted for another six hours, when he suddenly called out, "Something too awful has happened. My darling brother is dead." Then he muttered, "Who is that?" As he repeated the question his voice grew weaker and then was silenced. At 9:35 on the leaden morning of January 14, 1892, Prince Albert Victor, Duke of Clarence and Avondale—second in line to the throne of England, newly engaged, and just 28 years of age—was dead.[32]

In order to learn more about Eddy's illness, I studied the files of Dr. W. H. Broadbent, both at the Library of the New York Academy of Medicine and at the Wellcome Institute of the History of Medicine, London. I could not find any notes on his treatment of Prince Eddy. As an efficient and prominent physician to the Prince of Wales and to Queen Victoria, he would have followed standard clinical procedure and made notes about Prince Eddy's fatal illness. The only logical conclusion is that his clinical notes were removed, another example of the secrecy surrounding Eddy's life and death.

Reports that Eddy died from pneumonia and influenza might very well have been influenced by the fact that at that time there was an epidemic of influenza. However, the lightning abdominal pains he exhibited were not symptoms of pneumonia, but of neurosyphilis. Eddy also walked with a stiff, ataxic gait, assumed to have been caused by gout. But it is rare for a young man to have gout. His walking difficulties may have been rooted in his syphilitic illness. Syphilis, like diabetes, attacks every organ in the body, including the central and peripheral nervous systems. A recent article in the *New York State Journal of Medicine* noted, "The disease's manifestations are so diverse that syphilis has been called 'the great imposter' for its ability to mimic other diseases."[33]

The information we have on Eddy's illness comes from secondary sources. We don't have any reports from his attending physicians. However, I did locate a medical report on J. K.

My search for information on J. K.'s illness led me to St. Andrew's Hospital, Northampton, where J. K. had been a patient. I wrote to the medical director, Dr. J. H. Henderson, and he graciously and promptly sent me the summary report of J. K.'s admission and treatment at the hospital.[34]

JAMES KENNETH STEPHEN

Admitted 21st November 1891 under emergency order Aged 32, single. Barrister at Law of 18 Trinity Street. Cambridge, England. No previous treatment but said to have had a 'disease' affecting the mind since 1888. Present attack lasting 24 hours. Cause—blow on the head in 1887. Not thought to be suicidal or dangerous. No family history of insanity.

DIAGNOSIS

Extreme depression—almost mute. Has had episodes of depression lasting some weeks followed by periods of unusual excitability. This morning (at home) threw a looking glass into the street and stood naked in the window. Believed there was a warrant out for his detention.

STATE ON ADMISSION

Tall, well built, rather stout man in good physical health. His condition gradually improved and by 1st January 1892 he was described as being more cheerful and joining in activities. However on the 15th January he began refusing all food and had to be tube fed. This continued until 2nd Feburary when his physical condition collapsed and he died on 3rd Febuary 1892.

CAUSE OF DEATH

Mania
Refusal of food
Exhaustion

In modern terms it would seem that he suffered from Manic Depressive illness and this final episode was one of agitated depression with delusional ideas which gradually turned into a retarded depression with mutism and refusal of food.

The report confirmed a state of extreme depression which resulted in his death. I was delighted that the hospital had retained such records from the bygone century. I decided to visit the hospital with the optimistic prospect of uncovering further records of J. K.'s illness. Dr. Henderson was again amenable to assisting me.

The hospital is located in a large park, beautifully kept with large trees. I was guided through the facility and then to the room occupied by J. K. following the tour, Dr. Henderson placed before me a large portfolio containing the records of the patients in 1891, which included J. K. He was brought to the hospital by his older brother, Herbert Stephen, on November 21, 1891.

What is interesting to note here is that shortly before J. K.'s emergency admission to the hospital, he had been notified of Prince Eddy's intended marriage to Princess May. Eddy died on January 14, 1892. J. K. succumbed on February 3, 1892, within days of the date set for Eddy's marriage.

St. Andrew's Hospital, Northampton, England, where J. K. Stephen was treated and later died. (*Photo by the author, 1989*)

The hospital records were written by the hand of the medical superintendent at that time, who recorded the weekly reports on J. K.'s behavior related to him by medical attendants.[35] These reports provide valuable insight into J. K.'s mental decline. The minuscule penmanship is very difficult to read and I painstakingly attempted to decipher the handwriting. The full text is reprinted for the convenience of the reader.

Transcript of pages 172, 173 and 174 of Medical Protocol, St. Andrew's Hospital, Northampton, England

STEPHEN, JAMES KENNETH

Admitted November 21st 1891. Age 32 yrs & V mos. Single. Barrister at Law. Church of England. 18 Trinity St. Cambridge. First decided attack (but said to have been suffering from disease affecting mind since 1888). Never under treatment. Duration 24 hours. Supposed cause blow on head in January 1887. Not epileptic. Doubtful whether suicidal. Doubtful whether dangerous. No near relative afflicted with insanity. Usual Medical Attendant: Lawrence Humphrey M.D., 3 Trinity St. Cambridge.

Notice of death to brother (who signs order) Herbert Stephen. 32 DeVere Gardens, Kensington, London W.

MEDICAL STATEMENT:—

Extreme depression—often declining to speak or answer questions. This morning I found him standing naked in his bedroom, smiling. All the furniture & clothes in disorder & in the street were the fragments of looking glass which he had thrown from the window. He has had attacks of depression lasting for some months, followed by periods of unusual excitability: communicated by Harry Lushington Stephen, 32 DeVere Gardens, London, Barrister at Law. This morning in an attack of violence he threw his looking glass out of the window into the street & stood naked in his room & declined to move. Was under a delusion that there was a warrant out for his detention.

Lawrence Humphrey M.D.

STATE ON ADMISSION:—

He is tall, well-built & muscular, in good condition (inclined to be stout). There are no signs of recent disease or injury. Features regular. Eyes blue. Pupils equal, reaction to light normal. Complexion sallow. Hair dark brown. [unreadable, perhaps "thin on crown of head."] Face clean shaven. No organic disease of heart. Lungs sound. Abdominal organs apparently healthy. Tongue [perhaps "clear"]. Teeth somewhat defective. Pulse 104.

He arrived late at night & soon after admission went to his bath. At first he objected to bathe before "such a crowd"—myself & two attendants—& was somewhat slow & hesitating in undressing. Stated that there was nothing the matter with him except that he suffered from constipation & that opium was given to relieve this, but that it made him worse. Further than this he would say nothing & went to bed quietly. No 5. *C.O. Stanwell.*

November 22nd: His brother (Mr. Harry L. Stephen) spent the day with him. He was reserved, taciturn & almost silent all day, at times answering "Yes or No" to questions & at other times not speaking at all. He took a small amount of food at each meal. He spent all his time wandering about the garden or up & down his sitting room & would not [perhaps "read" or "amuse"] himself in any way. At bedtime he obstinately refused to go to bed & when an attempt was made to undress him he struck out at the attendant & had to be undressed & put to bed. When once in bed he was perfectly quiet. He was reported to have passed a quiet night & to have slept well. He was up this morning to breakfast with his brother. *C.O. Stanwell.*

November 23rd. He was yesterday visited by Messrs. Percival & Milligan, whose certificates are copied below; & today by Mr. Wm. Coulson, a Justice for the Borough of Northampton.

MEDICAL STATEMENTS:—

Very depressed, wanders disorderly about & will not amuse nor interest himself in anything. Obstinately refuses to answer any questions or to enter into conversation. His brother (Harry Lushington Stephen, Barrister, 32 DeVere Gardens, London W.) informs me: that he has delusions that there is a plot against him to deprive him of his liberty, that he made an indecent public speech & that he has committed some crime. He was sent for to Cambridge yesterday to see his brother, who had been in a violent state of excitement & destroyed his furniture & clothes, of which things the patient was afterwards unconscious.

G. H. Percival, M.B.

He appears to be very depressed: he absolutely refused to say a word to me & either sits staring moodily into the fire or walks up & down the room paying no attention to anything.

By his brother, Harry Lushington Stephen, 32 deVere Gardens, London W. Barrister. He informs me that his brother has for three years been subject to attacks & loss of self-control, followed by fits of depression & inaction. Yesterday at Cambridge he had an attack of mania, threw some of the furniture out of the room & stood naked for some time in a state of stupor. He has delusions that there is a plot to accuse him of a crime & that he made an indecent public speech.

Robert Arthur Milligan

November 25th: He is reported to have been quiet & to have slept well each night. He has had no action of the bowels since admission & on the 23rd refused to take any medicine. When threatened with the tube he took two pills (Hyd. Colsc. & Hyoscy:) [common prescriptions at that time for constipation and spasmodic stomach; these formulas are no longer used in modern treatment] followed after an interval by a dose of house mixture. This has had no effect & this afternoon he had an enema with only slight effect. His appetite is not good. He is reserved & taciturn, occasionally he will answer "Yes or No" but frequently will not speak. *C.O. Stanwell.*

December 2nd: He is quiet, very reserved, well conducted & giving no trouble. He takes exercise daily in the grounds & garden & when indoors spends all his time in his room reading. He is very quiet at night & reported to sleep well. He has a very fair appetite & is in good bodily health, though his bowels act very irregularly. He gives expression to no delusion & seldom says more than "Yes or No." *C.O. Stanwell.*

December 9th: Still reserved & quiet. Sits by himself all day when indoors usually reading. Quiet & giving no trouble. Seldom says more than "Yes or No" but appears to be comfortable & contented. Appetite good & in good bodily health. *C.O. Stanwell.*

December 16th: Very reserved & unsociable, though somewhat more cheerful. Reads a great deal. Takes country walks with his attendant. Apparently contented & giving no trouble. Seldom gets up in the morning till his breakfast is ready. Troubled a good deal with constipation, otherwise in good health. *C.O. Stanwell.*

December 23rd: He is unnaturally reserved, but more cheerful &

apparently contented. Will not take part in any amusement. Keeps entirely to himself & takes exercise in the country. His appetite is good & he is in good bodily health. Suffers somewhat from constipation & requires aperient medicine about twice a week. C.O. *Stanwell.*

1892 January 13th: Since last note he continued to improve, was more cheerful & sociable, playing billiards & taking regular exercise outside until the 10th. On the 9th he was visited by Lady Stephen & since then he has been very reserved & irritable. His appetite is poor, he will not go out, he reads very little, whereas before he used to read a great deal, he spends most of his time pacing up & down his room with his hands in his pockets. Frequently he will not answer a question. His bowels do not act at all regularly & tonight he threw two pills into the fire. This evening he would not allow his fire to be made up though the night is cold, & kept two windows in his room open. Except for the constipation he is in good bodily health. C.O. *Stanwell.*

January 18th: For the last three days he has taken no food & has been fed three times each day with the feeding tube. Yesterday & today he has struggled so violently that it is impossible to feed him by the mouth for fear of breaking his teeth when resisting to have the mouth open, [so] that he has been fed through the nose. Aperient medicine has been given but as this had no effect, today he had an enema with a fairly good result. He has been very violent to the attendants. He seldom speaks a word. Frequently out of bed standing on the floor or sitting on the edge of his bed. He was yesterday transferred to a warm room in the Infirmary from 4A where he had been in bed for three days. C.O. *Stanwell.*

January 21st: He is still refusing his food & is fed three times with the nasal tube. There has been no action of the bowels since the morning of the 18th after an enema. On external examination a collection of hard masses of faecal matter was found & this morning another enema was given & several large masses came away. When fed this afternoon a draught containing [perhaps "Tinct. Auri. Ore Aloes Co. & Tinct. Belladon"] was given, but at present has had no effect. He passes water in bed & while sitting in the chair for feeding & will not use the chamber utensil. Three letters have come for him from Lady Stephen (one yesterday & two today) but he will not open them. He offers little or no resistance before feeding but always tries to prevent the tube from passing by shaking his head & occasionally by coughing it into his mouth. Temperature 98.2. Pulse 96 & fairly good. C.O. Stanwell.

January 30th: He is still refusing his food & is being fed three times a day with the nasal tube. He has drunk one cup of tea & half a cup of coffee, but cannot be induced to take more. His strength is well maintained. C.O. Stanwell.

February 2nd: Yesterday & the day before he sucked the juice from an orange & today he has swallowed a very small quantity of brandy & water. Yesteday he suddenly became very much collapsed with a feeble pulse 123 & anxious expression, skin very dry, temp: 98°. Today he is very feeble, tongue dry & he swallows a small quantity of cold water with great difficulty. He has been fed daily with 2 eggs, $1/2$ pint milk & 2 oz Brandy morning & night & strong beef tea $1/2$ pint, 2 eggs & 2 oz. Port midday. Last night he had in addition to the eggs & milk a small teaspoonful of Liebigs extract of meat. At the midday feed today he vomited more than half back & was very much exhausted. This evening he has had one egg, 5 oz milk & 3 oz Brandy through the tube & has since been slightly better. His mouth has been washed out with weak Condy's fluid. The bowels have been acting fairly regularly lately & were open today, owing to small doses of Ext. Cascara Sagrada given night & morning. He has been very quiet & sleeps for a short time at intervals both night & day. C.O. Stanwell.

February 3rd: During last night he took a fair amount of nourishment: jelly, beeftea, 1 egg & brandy, though he swallowed with great difficulty. He frequently remarked "It's too late," when the feeding cup was put to his lips. He was visited by two brothers at 2 A.M. & talked to them. He remained conscious to within two hours of his death. At two thirty he became unconscious & sank rapidly. He died at 4.22 P.M. in the presence of his Mother (Lady Stephen), two brothers, myself & the Chief Attendant. C.O. Stanwell.

Statement of the cause of death.

James Kenneth Stephen died on the 3rd day of February 1892 at
4.22 P.M. in the presence of Edwin Cave, Chief Attendant. The
cause of death being:—Mania, Refusal of food, Exhaustion.

signed (signature unreadable)

Medical Superintendent

I noted that the staff had examined J. K.'s eyes as part of the
admission examination at St. Andrew's Hospital, Northampton.
The pupils were equal and reacted to light. This last finding—
that his pupils reacted to light—was important to learn because it
meant that J. K. presented no symptoms of any form of syphilis—
neither *tabes* nor general paralysis. In Dr. Stowell's report, as I
mentioned, it was unclear whether the patient was Eddy or J. K.
My findings show that the patient manifesting syphilitic symptoms
was Eddy.

The hospital record clearly reveals J. K.'s disturbed mental
condition. His morbid picture was greatly dominated by his depression and manic behavior. But this was partly obscured by his
impulsive reactions and marked lack of judgment—a behavior
carried out without consideration for others. The psychiatric report shows the high degree of care and treatment J. K. was given
by the hospital staff, and their understanding of his intricate
bodily and mental problems. Remembering that this report was
written a hundred years ago, at a time when psychiatry was in its
infancy, I was impressed by the patience and care with which the
staff treated a patient who behaved like a tormented bull.

Psychiatry has since that time made considerable progress in
delineating mental illnesses, and we are today able to identify
more accurately both J. K.'s symptoms and his behavior.

J. K. displayed a character disorder in his aggressive behavior
that expressed unconscious and conscious self-destructive tendencies, which manifested themselves in destroying others.

Persons having a character disturbance are not neurotic. Their

197

behavior and actions substitute for neurotic symptoms. These people are aggressive, assertive and anti-social and, at times, act irrationally.

People with character disorders commit all types of anti-social or criminal activities. In this group we find the rapist, the murderer, the pathological liar, the drug addict and the alcoholic. In the same group we also find very gifted, highly intelligent persons who commit criminal acts with great skill and adeptness and with much eccentricity. [36]

J. K.'s previously noted pronounced selfishness led him to feel superior and disdainful toward other people, in particular, women. Having achieved a prominent position at the university and in society, he unrealistically exaggerated his talent—his behavior becoming more pretentious and boisterous, seeking attention and admiration. Prone to impulsive reactions and rapid swings from elation to depression, his conduct was marked by criminal behavior, moral deficiency and sexual perversions. He would alternately suffer attacks of irritability, excitement and episodes of paranoia or confusion, which were symptomatic of his psychopathic personality and necrophiliac behavior. Since he was considered dangerous to others and to himself, the hospital administrators showed great wisdom in keeping him until the end.

The hospital report confirms that J. K. Stephen manifested symptoms of manic-depressive psychosis three years before he was institutionalized. That means he was insane at the time he committed the Whitechapel murders. During his manic ravings, he believed "there was a warrant out for his detention." [37]

The hospital termed it a delusion of a mentally ill patient. His statements that there was "a plot against him to deprive him of his liberty, that he had made an indecent public speech, and that he has committed some crime," reveal both his awareness of his sexual perversions and his overwhelming sense of guilt for his crimes. [38]

The Whitechapel murderer molested and desecrated the bodies

of his victims. Clearly, these mutilations showed his special enthu-
siasm and interest, indeed, his fondness, affection and even love
for the dead bodies. To be blunt, the Whitechapel murderer was
sexually in love with the lifeless bodies, which was the reason for
the mutilation. He could not give them up, surrender them to
somebody else. He wanted to possess their bodies. He put his mark
on them to show that they belonged to him and him alone. He was
now their master.

We may conclude that Jack the Ripper was sexually attracted to
corpses. He was a necrophiliac and committed necrophiliac murders. Necrophilia is a rare disorder recognized since olden times.
The seemingly innocuous story of "Sleeping Beauty" is an example
of necrophiliac fantasy. The common pattern for a necrophiliac is
first to make the victim defenseless or helpless, either by physical
assault or poisonous potion and then to kill her while she is
unconscious. This was also the method used by Jeffrey L. Dahmer
of Milwaukee, Wisconsin, who, in the course of about thirteen
years, allegedly killed and dismembered as many as seventeen boys
and young men.

The study of necrophiliac acts of serial murderers throws a
widening light on Jack the Ripper. The dead body provides the
necrophiliac murderer with the highest form of gratification.[39]
Such a murderer is overwhelmed by extreme destructive and sadistic desires. Jack the Ripper strangled his victims and then mutilated them. Deep in his mind he had felt rejected by women,
which is another way of saying he was afraid of them. One way of
getting rid of them was to kill them, or "plough them," as J. K.
wrote in a poem.

The necrophiliac murderer desires a sexual object, a woman or a
man unable to reject him. Killing women and then mutilating
them fulfilled that desire for Jack the Ripper. His fears turned into
desire and perverted love for his victims, once dead. In some cases,
such disturbed love goes as far as cannibalism, where one drinks
the blood or eats the flesh of the victim, as has been reported in

the case of Dahmer. To some extent, such was the case of Jack the Ripper.

J. K. and Eddy, acting in concert, are guilty of the Jack the Ripper murders. They were two strangers thrown together by fate and inclination, who shared life together as lovers and friends. J. K. played the role of leader, Eddy of follower. They also ended their lives together, barely three weeks apart.

Family backgrounds differed, but their emotional deprivation was quite similar. Love and security as they experienced them as children fell short of their needs. A proven principle of behavior is that human beings remain entrenched in the stage of growth where they have suffered emotional upset. Their bodies continue to grow, but their minds consistently relive the painful event while they desperately try to alter its outcome. All human conduct is symbolic of that episode revisited by the mind.

I am convinced that J.K. and Eddy were emotionally emasculated early in their childhood development. Their sexuality reached a certain degree of genital capacity, but it was lodged in the emotional preoccupations of a child. Their deviated sexuality was expressed in vengeful assaults on women. They were men who could feel no genital satisfaction with women. The knife symbolized a penetration more satisfying than sexual intercourse. I am also convinced that their childhood experiences resulted in the murder of their psyches, or souls.

Murder of children's souls is not a new phenomenon. It has been going on since the first child appeared on earth. When Freud originally described the psychological center of the person, he used the term "soul" (German, "seele"). Ibsen's accusation about "the murder of your soul" was apparently rooted in his own depressive, unhappy, tortuous childhood. I had uncovered his trauma through a dream he had when he was 13 or 14 years old. To my knowledge, it is the only dream of Ibsen's recorded. [40]

The psychodynamics of the Whitechapel murders are a good example of the effects of soul murder. Both perpetrators, J. K. and

Eddy, developed as paraphiliac persons whose loving ability had been arrested or otherwise damaged. Fearing normal adult sexual encounters, they preferred less threatening sexual activities with children or homosexuals, and sometimes resigned themselves to the company of prostitutes. The physical destruction of the prostitutes provided sexual stimulation as well as vengeance for their own soul murders.

The intimacy shared by J. K. and Prince Eddy was deeply rooted. One is left with the impression that, even when physically separated from each other, each knew practically all the time where the other one was.

It was no coincidence that their lives came to an end around the same time. Prince Eddy died January 14, 1892. J. K. followed on February 3, 1892. Two men of staunch power were brought low. J. K. once described himself in one of his poems as a pillar of society.

> I have no time to tell you how
> I came to be a killer
> But you should know, as time will show,
> That I'm society's pillar.[41]

Eddy, perhaps, still fantasized that one day he would become King. Neither one could realize his dream. Faced with defeat, their only power lay in designing their own deaths. What appeared on the surface to be death from a mental or physical illness went far beyond that.

All murderers are preoccupied with death—not only for their victims, but also for themselves. Certain unconscious fears urge them toward self-destruction. In order to avoid marriage, Eddy may have unconsciously exposed himself to syphilis and his eventual demise. J. K. retreated into mental delusion as a form of suicidal withdrawal from his life. Both became their own victims of death. And both remained united in their self-murders.

201

Prince Eddy and J. K. Stephen were victims but so were those who raised them. In a significant way, we are all victims of victims.

1. Thomas E. A. Stowell, M.D., "Jack the Ripper. A Solution?," *The Criminologist*, November, 1970, p. 47.
2. *Ibid.*
3. *Ibid.*
4. *Ibid.*, pp. 49–50.
5. *Ibid.*, p. 50.
6. *Ibid.*
7. *Ibid.*, p. 47.
8. *Ibid.*
9. *Ibid.*
10. *Ibid.*
11. *Ibid.*
12. Martin Howells and Keith Skinner, *The Ripper Legacy: The Life and Death of Jack the Ripper*, Sidgwick & Jackson, London, 1987, pp. 162–163.
13. *Ibid.*
14. James Edmund Vincent, *His Royal Highness the Duke of Clarence and Avondale: A Memoir*, Murray, London, 1893, p. 19.
15. *Ibid.*, p. 261.
16. *Ibid.*
17. Michael Harrison, *Clarence, the Life of H.R.H. The Duke of Clarence and Avondale*, W. H. Allen, London, 1972, p. 222.
18. Anne Edwards, *Matriarch*, William Morrow & Company, New York, 1984, p. 54.
19. Richard Gordon, *Jack the Ripper*, Atheneum, New York, 1980, p. 186.
20. Medical Admission Protocol, St. Andrew's Hospital, Northampton, England, 1892.
21. Michael Harrison, *op. cit.*
22. Medical Admission Protocol, *op. cit.*
23. *Ibid.*
24. Virginia Woolf, *Moments of Being. Unpublished Autobiographical*

Writings, edited with introduction and notes by Jeanne Schulkind, Harcourt Brace Jovanovich, New York and London, 1976, pp. 98–99.

25. Louise De Salvo, *Virginia Woolf: The Impact of Childhood Sexual Abuse on Her Life and Work*, Beacon Press, Boston, 1989, p. 145.

26. David Abrahamsen, *The Mind of the Accused: A Psychiatrist in the Courtroom*, Simon & Schuster, New York, 1983, p. 47.

27. Martin Howells and Keith Skinner, *op. cit.*, p. 160.

28. Thomas Stowell, *op. cit.*, p. 48.

29. Anne Edwards, *op. cit.*, pp. 54–55.

30. *Ibid.*, p. 55.

31. Israel S. Wechsler, *A Textbook of Clinical Neurology*, Fourth edition, W.B. Saunders Company, Philadelphia, PA, 1939, p. 475. Dr. S.A. Vinnie Wilson, *Neurology*, Volume I, Classics of Neurosurgery Library, London, 1989.

32. Anne Edwards, *op. cit.*, p. 85.

33. *New York State Journal of Medicine*, Vol. 9, No. 12, December, 1991.

34. Medical Admission Protocol, *op. cit.*

35. *Ibid.*

36. David Abrahamsen, *The Psychology of Crime*, Columbia University Press, New York, 1960, pp. 134–144.

37. Medical Admission Protocol, *op. cit.*

38. *Ibid.*

39. Jonathan Rosman, M.D. and Philip Resnick, "Sexual Attraction to Corpses; Psychiatric Review of Necrophilia," *Psychiatry Law*, Vol. 17, No. 2, 1989, pp. 153–163.

40. David Abrahamsen, *Henrik Ibsen's Personality Illuminated Through a Dream*, Ibsen Association Yearbook, 1952, reprinted, New York, 1990.

41. Michael Harrison, *op. cit.*, p. 189.

Bibliography

Abrahamsen, David, M.D., F.A.C.Pn., *Crime and the Human Mind*. New York: Columbia University Press, 1944.

_____. *The Mind and Death of a Genius*, New York: Columbia University Press, 1986.

_____. *Henrik Ibsen's Personality Illuminated Through a Dream*. Ibsen Association Yearbook, New York, 1952.

_____. *The Road to Emotional Maturity*, New York: Prentice Hall, 1958.

_____. *The Psychology of Crime*. New York: Columbia University Press, 1960.

_____. "The Harvey Oswald Psychological Capacity for Violence and Murder." *Bulletin* of the New York Academy of Medicine, vol. 43, no. 10, pp. 861–888 (October, 1967).

_____. *Our Violent Society*. New York: Funk & Wagnalls, 1970.

_____. *The Murdering Mind*. New York: Harper & Row, 1973.

_____. *The Emotional Care of Your Child*. New York: Simon & Schuster, 1974.

_____. *Nixon vs. Nixon*. New York: Farrar Straus & Giroux, 1977.

_____. "Mass Murderers, Son of Sam and Jack the Ripper." XII Congress of the International Academy of Forensic and Social Medicine, Vienna, August, 1982.

_____. *The Mind of the Accused: A Psychiatrist in the Courtroom*. New York: Simon & Schuster, 1983.

_____. *Confessions of Son of Sam*. New York: Columbia University Press, 1985.

Acton, William. *Prostitution, Considered in its Moral, Social, and Sanitary Aspects, in London and Other Large Cities and Garrison Towns, with Proposals for the Control and Prevention of its Attendant Evils*. London: John Churchill, 1862.

Annan, Noel Gilroy. *Leslie Stephen, His Thoughts and Character in Relationship to His Time*. Cambridge: Harvard University Press, 1952.

Aronson, Theo. *The King in Love*. New York: Harper & Row, 1959.

Ars Quatuor Coronatorum, Lodge 2076, Vol. 99, Adlaird & Son, London, September, 1987.

Battiscombe, Georgina. *Queen Alexandra*. Boston: Houghton Mifflin Co., 1969.

Bell, Quentin. *Virginia Woolf: A Biography*. New York: Harcourt Brace Jovanovich, 1972.

Benson, Arthur Christopher. *The Leaves of the Tree: Studies in Biography*. London: G. P. Putnam's Sons, 1911.

Biggs, Lt. Michael E. *Escort Services: A Front for Prostitution, F.B.I. Law Enforcement Bulletin*, August, 1988.

Bloch, Michael. *The Duke of Windsor's War*. New York: Weidenfeld & Nicolson, 1982.

Broadbent, Sir William. *Life of Sir William Broadbent, Bart., K.C.V.O., Physician Extraordinary to H. M. Queen Victoria*. Edited by M. E. Broadbent. London: John Murray, 1909.

Bibliography

Cambridge Review, February, 1891.

Camps, Francis E., Professor, *London Hospital Gazette*, Vol. LXIX, No. 1, April 1966.

Clark, Louise, *How to Recognize and Overcome Dyslexia in Your Child*, Dagbladeb (Daily Newspaper), Oslo, September 18, 1990.

Clear, Celia. *Royal Children from 1840–1980*. London: Arthur Barker, 1981.

Deacon, Richard. *The Cambridge Apostles: A History of Cambridge University's Elite Intellectual Secret Society*.

De Salvo, Louise. *Virginia Woolf: The Impact of Childhood Sexual Abuse on Her Life and Work*. Boston: Beacon Press, 1989.

Dickens, Charles. *Bleak House*. London: Bradbury and Evans, 1853.

Donaldson, Frances. *Edward VIII*. New York: Weidenfeld & Nicolson, 1974.

Eckert, William G., M.D. "The Whitechapel Murders: The Case of Jack the Ripper." *The American Journal of Forensic Medicine and Pathology*, vol. 2, no. 1, March, 1981.

Edwards, Ann. *Matriarch: Queen Mary and the House of Windsor*. New York: William Morrow and Co., 1984.

Evans, B.I., *English Poetry in the Later Nineteenth Century*, University College, London, 1966.

Fogel, Gerald I., M.D., and Wayne A. Myers, M.D., *Perversions and Near Perversions in Clinical Practice: New Psychoanalytic Perspectives*, New Haven: Yale University Press, 1991.

Freud, Sigmund, M.D., Lecture, *Archiv fur Kriminalanthropologie und Kriminalstatistik*, von H. Gross, BD. 26, 1906.

_____. *Collected Papers*. London: Hogarth Press, 1942.

Gordon, Richard. *Jack the Ripper*. New York: Atheneum, 1980.

Goring, Charles. *The English Convict*. Prison Commission, London, 1913.

Gull, William Withey, Bart., M.D., F.R.S. *A Collection of the Published Writings of William Withey Gull, Bart., M.D., F.R.S.* Edited by Theodore Dyke Acland. London: The New Sydenham Society, 1896.

Harrison, Michael. *The Life of H.R.H. The Duke of Clarence and Avondale*. London: W. H. Allen, 1972.

Haslam, Anthony D. *James Kenneth Stephen*. 1986. Unpublished paper.

Howells, Martin, and Keith Skinner. *The Ripper Legacy: The Life and Death of Jack the Ripper*. London: Sidgwick & Jackson, 1987.

Kelly, Alexander. *A Bibliography and Review of the Literature*. London: Association of Assistant Librarians, S.E.D., 1973.

Knight, Stephen. "Jack the Ripper: The Final Solution," *The Criminologist*, November, 1976.

Larkins, E. K., Esq. *The Whitechapel Murders 1888*. Collected Evidence, London, 1888.

London, Jack. *The People of the Abyss*. New York: Macmillan & Co., 1903.

Magnus, Philip. *King Edward, the Seventh*. London: John Murray, 1964.

Mayhew, Henry. *London's Underworld*. London: William Kimber & Co., 1862.

"Queen Victoria's Medical Household," *Medical History, A Quarterly Journal Devoted to the History of Medicine and Related Sciences*, Vol. 26, London: Wellcome Institute for the History of Medicine, 1982.

206

INDEX